FRONT COVER

Adelicia Hayes Franklin Acklen sat for the portrait Adelicia Franklin with Horse Bucephalus during her first marriage. Her great-granddaughter remembered, "Unlike some ladies, grandmother liked to take the reins and drive even the most spirited animals," and it was said that she would rather jump over a closed gate than stop to open it. (William Browning Cooper, artist, ca. 1840, Belmont Mansion Association)

BACK COVER

Adelicia Acklen's magnificent Belmont estate included formal landscaping over about sixty of its 177 acres. Many in the 1850s considered the mansion on the hill the most magnificent in the South. (View of Belmont, ca. 1860, Belmont Mansion Association)

VOLUME LXXVI SPRING 2017 NUMBER 1

A publication of the Tennessee Historical Society in cooperation with the Tennessee Historical Commission.

2	**Adelicia Acklen:** Beyond the "Belmont" Legend and Lore BY BRENDA JACKSON-ABERNATHY
44	**Belmont Mansion:** An Icon of the American Country House Movement BY JERRY TRESCOTT
80	**"Making a Display":** Adelicia Acklen's Tennessee Family Portraits BY RACHEL STEPHENS
102	**Grounds of "Improvement":** The Belmont Mansion Garden BY JUDY BULLINGTON
127	**Contributors**
128	**Guidelines**

The *Tennessee Historical Quarterly* (ISSN 0400–3261) is published quarterly for $35 per year by the Tennessee Historical Society, 305 6th Ave. North, War Memorial Building, Nashville, TN 37243–0084. Periodicals postage paid at Nashville, TN.

Correspondence concerning subscriptions or membership should be addressed to Membership Director, Tennessee Historical Society, 305 6th Ave. North, Nashville, TN 37243–0084. Phone: 615–741–8934. This number may be obtained at $15.00 per copy, plus tax and postage, if applicable.

POSTMASTER: Send address changes to the Tennessee Historical Society, 305 6th Ave. North, Nashville, TN 37243–0084.

Correspondence concerning contributions and manuscripts for the quarterly should be addressed to Kristofer Ray, Editor, P.O. Box 89, Post Mills, VT 05058 Kristofer.Ray@dartmouth.edu.

The Tennessee Historical Commission and the Tennessee Historical Society disclaim responsibility for statements, whether fact or of opinion, made by contributors.

Copyright ©2017 by The *Tennessee Historical Society*

ADELICIA ACKLEN:
Beyond the "Belmont" Legend and Lore

BY BRENDA JACKSON-ABERNATHY

Adelicia Acklen. To many Tennesseans, the name is a familiar one, though they may not know why. Some may recall traveling the Nashville city streets that bear her name, or be familiar with the large Italian Villa-style mansion at the center of the Belmont University campus that was once her home. Others may know the stories casting Acklen as Nashville's own Scarlett O'Hara during the Civil War, but beyond the landmarks and legends, most know very little of this woman and the role she played in Nashville and Civil War history.

Adelicia Acklen's relative anonymity is curious until a concerted search for documents, records, and other "verifiable evidence" of her life and activities is launched. Common sense would suggest the existence of plentiful records left by the woman who built the Belmont Mansion and owned its surrounding acreage, as well as nearly ten thousand acres of agricultural land in Louisiana, and other assorted parcels in various southern states. Certainly deeds, bills of sale, receipts, and the accompanying correspondence necessary to conduct business and maintain properties and estates as extensive as these were carefully preserved during Acklen's lifetime, and neatly tucked away in well-organized and accessible archival collections after her death. That scenario is reasonable, and makes sense, but the fact is, this cache of personal papers and documents of which historians and researchers dream no longer exists, or if it does, has not come to light. The possibilities of just what happened to Adelicia Acklen's personal papers are numerous—perhaps, Acklen purged her personal files over the years; perhaps, following her death her children disposed of paperwork for which they saw no practical need; perhaps, as Belmont passed into the hands of others, documents and papers in which they had no interest were simply destroyed. Whatever the case, Acklen's surviving personal papers are few, housed in collections scattered across the country, and

One of the wealthiest women in the United States from the 1840s until her death in 1887, Adelicia Acklen created Belmont as a summer pleasure estate. By 1860, Belmont became the showplace of Nashville. (Portrait by Washington Bogart Cooper, early 1850s, Belmont Mansion Association)

their scarcity makes writing a biographical study of her life nearly impossible. Her story, though, pasted together with the documents that do exist, causes the task to be worthy of the challenge, for through it the life of an elite white woman in Nashville's early days of growth and expansion is better understood. In particular, her actions during the Civil War in Nashville and in Louisiana reveal the tenacity and determination of a Southern woman to take whatever steps necessary to preserve hearth, home, and the wellbeing of those who depended on her—in Acklen's case, that number topped eight hundred individuals.

The narrative that follows, then, is not the consummate biographical study on Adelicia Acklen; rather, it is a glimpse into the life of one of Nashville's most interesting female characters. Utilizing those Acklen primary sources that do exist, and relying on Nashville legend and lore to fill in the gaps, the goal is to give a face to the name, and an appreciation for the woman who built the big pink house on the hill.

Adelicia Acklen was born Adelicia Hayes, on March 15, 1817—the Ides of March—in Nashville, Tennessee. Her father, Oliver Bliss Hayes, a New Englander by birth, left his Massachusetts home in the first years of the nineteenth century to pursue a career in the law—first in Baltimore, and later in Nashville—and established himself in the profession Anita Shafer Goodstein suggests "carried the greatest weight and opened the most doors."[1] Her mother's family migrated from North Carolina to Williamson County, Tennessee, probably in the late 1780s, where Adelicia's grandfather, Richard Hightower, is remembered as a founding member of the county.[2] Her mother, Sarah Hightower, was noted for her beauty, and artist Ralph E. W. Earl remarked he had "never painted a portrait from a lovelier model,"[3] when she sat for him in the early 1810s. On February 2, 1812, Oliver Hayes and Sarah Hightower married,[4] and over the next five years welcomed the first three of their eventual ten children into the family: two sons, Richard Hightower Hayes and Joel Addison Hayes, and in 1817, a daughter, Adelicia, whose dark-haired loveliness certainly favored her mother.

By the time of Adelicia's birth in the late 1810s, Middle Tennessee had experienced tremendous economic and population growth, and was no longer the isolated frontier community founded by James Robertson and John Donelson in 1780.[5] A concerted focus on land speculation and tobacco and cotton production increased trade and brought new groups of settlers to Middle Tennessee, eager to capitalize on the promise of lucrative opportunities available there. When Adelicia turned three, in 1820, the region's population topped 290,000,[6] signaling not only a significant increase in numbers, but a change in the population make-up as well. As Kristofer Ray has pointed out, in addition to the yeoman farmers and speculators who first settled in and around Nashville, "now there was a diverse economic population that included merchants, planters, and intraregional commercial interests."[7] Consider "intraregional commercial interests" as code for "cotton," for as Ray further suggests, "when cotton emerged as a viable commodity," particularly in Nashville, the principle port on the Cumberland River, "progressive planters, lawyers, and merchants became boosters to that crop and of the small town."[8]

Oliver Hayes belonged to this booster group and practiced law in early Nashville with some of the era's giants; Thomas H. Benton, Felix Grundy, and "Old Hickory" himself, Andrew Jackson, among them. He argued numerous land dispute cases, and participated in several of Nashville's most important federal cases, including the request, in the spring of 1819, that a branch of the Bank of the United States be opened in Nashville, ultimately denied by the bank's president, Langdon Cheves.[9] In addition to his legal endeavors, Hayes engaged in a variety of business pursuits in and around Nashville and Middle Tennessee ranging from real estate promotion, to partnership in a local paper mill, and serving on numerous Boards of Directors.[10] Hayes also participated in Nashville's philanthropic and community organizations, held membership in Hiram Lodge No. 7, F&AM, and served in 1819 as Grand Master of the Grand Lodge of Tennessee.[11]

His varied and lucrative business pursuits allowed Oliver Hayes to establish a comfortable home and lifestyle for his growing family, and Adelicia spent her first few years in the Nashville home her grandfather Hightower presented to her parents as a wedding gift. Located on High Street, in close proximity to what is now the corner of Union and Sixth Avenue North, the red brick, two-story home was comprised "of a number of old-fashioned large rooms with high ceilings and big fireplaces,"[12] surrounded by "ornamental grounds"[13] and was "full of life and gaiety"[14] while Oliver and Sarah Hayes, and their four eldest children resided there.[15]

Hayes family lore suggests a close and loving relationship existed between Adelicia and her father, and his actions in furthering women's education in young Nashville make clear his desire and determination she receive a classical education, as rigorous as that provided her brothers. On August 4, 1817, the Nashville Female Academy opened its doors,[16] with Oliver B. Hayes[17] among the original "subscribers," and a member of the Board of Trustees from 1819 until at least 1826.[18] Adelicia's name appears on surviving documents from as early as 1825, indicating she began her formal education at eight years of age, or younger. She was an above-average student, and according to the "Bill of Recitations" for the academic year ending in June of 1827, when she was ten years old, earned 565 "perfect" points out of a possible 600.[19] Adelicia attended school with the daughters of Nashville's elite and well-connected, and the names Grundy, Robertson, McGavock, and McNairy are common on the academy's roll. While all indicators suggest Oliver Hayes stepped away from his position as

In the 1830s, Adelicia Hayes became engaged to the law student Alfonso Gibbs. Grief and mourning replaced wedding and trousseau preparation when Gibbs died in October 1834. (Portrait by Washington Bogart Cooper, ca. 1834, Belmont Mansion Association)

academy trustee after 1826, educating his daughters remained a priority, and an 1839 academy roster lists Adelicia's younger sister, Laura, among its students.[20]

In the mid-1820s, in order to accommodate his growing family, Oliver Hayes acquired the Rokeby estate in Nashville, comprised of two 640-acre military land grants[21] and a house described as "massive" and "palatial," with a front door large enough to allow "a carriage and pair" to pass. The happiest years were certainly those when the Hayes children were in residence, and it was said "during their tenure of the old house at Rokeby it was the scene of constant gayety." It is certain the home was the site of parties, dances, and teas in abundance, as "gallants flocked a-courting there the three fair maids of Rokeby," referring to Adelicia and her sisters, Laura and Corinne.[22] Rokeby may well have witnessed the initial meeting between Adelicia Hayes and her first serious beau, for at some point in the early 1830s she made the acquaintance of Alphonso Gibbs, eldest son of George and Lee Ann Dibrell Gibbs. The Gibbs family relocated to Nashville from North Carolina, probably in the mid-1810s. George Gibbs practiced law and worked in banking, and certainly became acquainted with Oliver Hayes through these endeavors, perhaps leading to the introduction of the young couple.

Five years Hayes's senior, Alphonso Gibbs planned to follow his father into a career in the law and, once established, marry the lovely Adelicia.[23] His dreams of a successful and lucrative law practice, and theirs of a long and happy life together were left unfulfilled, however, as Gibbs contracted typhoid fever, left Harvard prior to completing his studies in the spring or summer of 1834,[24] and died that October.[25] Grief and mourning replaced wedding and trousseau preparation for seventeen-year-old Hayes, and included in the scattered collections containing her documents is a revision of a poem written by Amelia Opie and published earlier in 1834, in a collection entitled *Lays for The Dead*.[26] Admittedly, Hayes took poetic license with Opie's poem and re-worked a number of its stanzas, but through these lines her thoughts on Gibbs's passing, and what life might hold for her are clearly revealed:

> There was an eye whose partial glance,
> Could ne'er my numerous faults see;
> There was an ear that still untried,
> Could listen to kind praise of me.
>
> There was a heart time only made,
> I or me with fonder feelings burn.
> And which, where'er alas! I moved,
> Still long and pined for my return.
>
> There was a lip which always breathed
> E'en short farewells with tones of sadness;
> There was a voice whose eager sound,
> My welcome spoke with heartfelt gladness.
>
> There was a mind whose vigorous powers,
> On mine their fostering influence threw;
> and called my humble talents forth,
> Till thence its dearest joys it drew.
>
> There was a love which oft for me,
> With anxious fears would overflow;
> And wept and prayed for me, and sought
> From future ills to guard—but now!
>
> That eye is closed and deaf that ear,
> That lip and voice are mute forever;
> And cold that heart of faithful love,
> Which death alone from mine could sever.
>
> And lost to me that ardent mind,
> Which loved my varied task to see;
> And oh, of all the praise I gained,
> This was the dearest for to me!
>
> Now I, unloved, uncherished, alone,
> Life's weary wilderness must tread;
> Till he who heals the broken heart,
> In mercy bids me join the dead.
>
> But, "Father of the Fatherless,"
> Oh thou that hear'est the orphan's cry,
> And dwellest with the contrite heart,
> As well as in thy place on high.
>
> Oh, Lord! Though like a faded leaf,
> That's severed from its parent tree,
> I struggle down life's stormy tide,
> That awful tide which leads to thee.
>
> Still, Lord! To thee the voice of praise,
> Shall spring triumphant from my breast;
> Since though I tread a weary way,
> I trust that he I mourn is blest!
>
> —Adelicia

It seems Hayes mourned Alphonso Gibbs for some time, and not until about 1837 did she meet Isaac Franklin, the man who became her first husband. The exact date of this meeting is not known, but as the story goes, Hayes was in Gallatin, Tennessee, visiting her father's first cousin, Judge John J. White, and his wife, Catherine "Kitty" Waide. During her stay, the Whites suggested a visit to the stately Fairvue mansion so she might see its recent additions, and perhaps meet its owner.[27] According to some accounts, Isaac Franklin was not at home when Hayes and the Whites called, so they were asked to sign the guest register, and here the "legend" takes on a life of its own. According to one source, when Hayes expressed her disappointment at missing Franklin, the butler responded she would not have "caught" him anyway, causing Hayes to inscribe next to her name, "I like this house. I'd like to meet the owner."[28] A more recent source omits discussion of the butler altogether, crediting a bold Adelicia Hayes with writing after her name, "I like this house and set my cap for its master."[29] As the Fairvue guest register is lost to history, Hayes's inscription—if she left one at all—will never be known, though it is highly unlikely she left either of the messages noted above, both of which were inappropriate at the time for a woman of her standing. In her son William Hayes Ackland's telling of the tale, Franklin was at Fairvue on the day in question, and offered his visitors a personally-guided tour of the house. Ackland's[30] version may hold more validity than some of the others as he no doubt heard his mother retell the story at various times throughout his life. To continue, when the house tour reached the drawing room, Franklin asked "if he might not hear a song," as was customary for the time, and Hayes with "a voice of remarkable sweetness" according to her son, sang the popular "Buds and Flowers." Apparently, that was all it took and the "old bachelor's heart... capitulated at once."[31] Whether it was the sweet voice, bold message, or some combination of these qualities, this event appears to be the beginning of the romance that led, on July 1, 1839, to the marriage of Isaac Franklin and Adelicia Hayes, solemnized by J.T. Edgar, pastor at Nashville's First Presbyterian Church.[32]

Isaac Franklin was an intriguing "love interest" choice for Hayes, now Adelicia Franklin. He did number among the most eligible bachelors in Middle Tennessee, perhaps in the South, in the 1830s, but he and Gibbs could not have been more different, which makes the relationship all the more interesting. Where Gibbs was Hayes's contemporary in terms of age and education, at the time of their eventual meeting Franklin was in his late forties to Hayes's early twenties and had the benefit of only the most rudimentary education. An attractive man with dark hair and eyes, evidenced by surviving portraits, he was very wealthy and in addition to the 2,000-acre Sumner County, Tennessee, property which housed Fairvue, owned close to 8,000 acres planted in cotton in Louisiana's West Feliciana Parish, as well as property in Mississippi and Texas. While his wealth, and the promise of the life she would enjoy as Mrs. Franklin, may have aided in Hayes's decision to accept Franklin's marriage proposal, he must have possessed other qualities that appealed to her. Those, of course, and her thoughts on the matter are also lost to history.

After a honeymoon lasting most of the summer, and visits to the Atlantic seaboard and other locations, the Franklins returned to Fairvue and began their married life in

In 1837, Adelicia Hayes met Isaac Franklin, owner of magnificent Fairvue in Sumner County. They married in 1839; Franklin likely added the wing to the right at the time of their marriage. (HABS, 1936, Library of Congress)

late 1839.[33] While the house itself was spectacular, described by Caroline Seebohm and Peter Woloszynski in *Under Live Oaks, The Last Great Houses of the Old South* as "a two-story brick structure with Georgian and Greek Revival flourishes," and "Irish Kilkenny marble mantels and furnishing from New Orleans,"[34] it was located in rural Sumner County, a good distance from the bustling activity of Nashville, and it likely took Adelicia Franklin some time to become accustomed to the slower pace of rural life.

A bit about Isaac Franklin is important here—his beginnings, his business interests, his accumulation of wealth—for without Franklin, Adelicia would not have acquired such vast resources and her life would certainly have taken very different turns. Isaac Franklin's ties to Middle Tennessee date

In 1836, the American Anti-Slavery Society targeted Franklin & Armfield and their "private prison" for slaves pending sale in Alexandria. In 1834 alone, the firm stated that they shipped "not less than 1000 slaves" to New Orleans. (Detail from "Slave Market of America," 1836, Library of Congress)

to the original American settlement of the region, as his father James Franklin was part of the 1780 expedition lead by Kasper Mansker that arrived in what became Sumner County.[35] The elder Franklin also numbered among the "immortal seventy," named by Nashville founder James Robertson in a 1784 Act passed by the North Carolina General Assembly that granted six hundred and forty acres of land to those involved in the "defence [sic] and settlement of the said county of Davidson."[36] With this grant, James Franklin secured land at Pilot Knob on Station Camp Creek, and began construction of the home and farm that supported the family for many years. Isaac Franklin was born in 1789, just three years after work on this home began, the sixth of ten children born to James and Mary Lauderdale Franklin.[37]

Isaac Franklin left no recollections or reminiscences of his youth, but he probably spent those long spring and summer days hunting and fishing with his brothers and assisting his father farming the family's substantial holdings. Mary Franklin would have provided her children with the basics of reading, writing, and arithmetic, and they may have attended a country day school from time to time. In his teen-age years, Franklin worked with his older brothers in merchandising endeavors—transporting product from the agricultural regions of Tennessee downriver to markets in Natchez and New Orleans, "a pursuit open only at that day to the most adventurous of the people,"[38] the *Mississippi Free Trader* declared years later at Franklin's death. The War of 1812 temporarily interrupted Franklin's business endeavors, and he spent at least its latter years as Second Lieutenant, Second Regiment Mounted Gunmen, West Tennessee Volunteers,[39] reinforcing Andrew Jackson's troops in their battles with the Creeks in Alabama.[40]

After the war, Franklin returned to Sumner County and established himself on five hundred acres of prime agricultural land, purchased from and gifted by his father.[41] At about the same time, he began to augment his wealth using trading skills honed earlier, this time through the domestic slave trade. Franklin's pre-war years on the river undoubtedly introduced him to the trade and its growth following the 1808 abolition of the international slave trade. As well, Franklin certainly knew the vast, fertile lands brought into the United States with the Louisiana Purchase had created a massive southward movement of agriculturalists in search of a labor force.[42] Although his involvement may have begun sooner, the Adams County, Mississippi, records from 1819 are the earliest to definitively show Franklin buying and selling slaves in the Natchez market,[43] and his increased involvement in the trade is confirmed with the 1823 purchase of a parcel of property located just east of downtown Natchez, at the "Forks of the Road."[44] As demand for slaves grew, so did Franklin's enterprise, and on February 28, 1828, he formed a partnership with John Armfield, with whom he had worked since 1824.[45] With operations based in Alexandria, Virginia, where Armfield acquired the slaves Franklin then sold to Louisiana and Mississippi planters, Franklin and Armfield soon became the largest and most profitable slave-trading enterprise in the country.

The image most often painted of the early nineteenth-century slave trader reveals a sinister and dastardly fellow, a pariah, an individual shunned by polite society—unless labor needs necessitated his services. A question to consider here, then: are these "images" appropriate when considering early-nineteenth century society; and if so, why in the world did Oliver B. Hayes allow Adelicia, his favored eldest daughter, to marry such an individual? The observations of northern writer Joseph Holt

Ingraham may be instructive here, for he visited the Forks of the Road slave market in the mid-1830s, and wrote about the people he observed there. It is likely the following remarks refer to Isaac Franklin:

> Negro traders soon accumulate great wealth, from the immense profit they make on their merchandise… One of their number, who is the great southern slave-merchant, and who, for the last fifteen years, has supplied this country with two-thirds of the slaves brought into it, has amassed a fortune of more than a million of dollars by this traffic alone. He is a bachelor, and a man of gentlemanly address, as are many of these merchants, not the ferocious, Captain Kidd looking fellows, we Yankees have been apt to imagine them. Their admission into society, however, is not recognized. Planters associate with them freely enough, in the way of business, but notice them no further.[46]

So, according to Ingraham, Franklin's physical appearance was not that of a scourge of society; his last comment, though, is particularly interesting and reflects the thoughts of many scholars concerning the relationships between slaveholders and other members of polite society, and slave traders. Others, though, rebut the idea of the slave trader as a societal outcast and maintain white Southerners were content, and not uncomfortable, with the trade or the trader.[47] This later suggestion, argued by Michael Tadman and others, makes the Franklin-Hayes union, and particularly Oliver B. Hayes's approval of it, make much more sense.

Franklin and Armfield delivered a great deal of wealth to Isaac Franklin, of that there is no doubt, but it is also clear Franklin did not intend to remain in the trade indefinitely. By the mid-1830s he had purchased several hundred acres of land in Louisiana's West Feliciana Parish,[48] and by 1834 was living there for at least a portion of the year.[49] While Franklin does not state his reasons for divesting himself of his partnership interest and retiring from the trade, the economic downtown of 1837 certainly factored into the decision, and by the time of his marriage to Hayes in 1839, he was active only in collecting unpaid debuts. By 1841, the partnership of Franklin and Armfield was dissolved,[50] and Franklin's time dedicated to that of full-time planter.

Throughout their married life, the Franklins split their time between Fairvue and the Louisiana plantations, summering in the former and wintering in the latter. The Louisana residence was quite modest, not nearly as grand as Fairvue; a wood structure described at the time of Franklin's death as "old and the galleries somewhat decayed." Franklin intended to build a new and more spacious Louisiana home for his growing family, had selected the location and contracted with a carpenter to begin once his current project was completed.[51] Time in Louisiana was not all spent on the plantations, though, and included extended

Adelicia and Isaac Franklin had four children between 1840 and 1844. Washington B. Cooper completed this portrait of the three Franklin girls, Victoria, Adelicia, and Emma, in 1845, only nine months before the death of the two older girls in 1846. (Belmont Mansion Association)

trips to New Orleans, dedicated to both business and pleasure. And despite the difference in their ages, the Franklin marriage was apparently a happy one, with children born in rather rapid succession: Victoria in the spring of 1840, Adelicia in 1842, Julius, who lived just two days, in January of 1844, and Emma, in December of 1844. This idyllic family picture was not to last, however, for in the spring of 1846, Franklin became ill with a stomach complaint, and on April 27, just a month prior to his fifty-seventh birthday, he died on the Louisiana plantation.[52] Plans were immediately made to return his body to Sumner County, with Adelicia Franklin, her father, and the children accompanying Franklin on his final journey home. This episode proved devastating to Adelicia for reasons beyond Franklin's death, as both Victoria and little Adelicia became ill and shortly after returning to Fairvue died within three days of each other, on June 11 and June 8, respectively. Their obituary in the *Nashville Union* recalled of the little girls, "their intellectual and moral developments were remarkable for their age, and none were ever more lovely and promising."[53] With her seventh wedding anniversary just weeks away, in July of 1846, Franklin found herself widowed and no doubt holding tight to Emma, her sole surviving child. The two spent a good amount of time following their loss with Adelicia's parents at Rokeby in Nashville, as well as at Fairvue. The Louisiana plantations were under the care and direction of overseers and managers, with her father, Oliver B. Hayes, and John Armfield, executors of Franklin's estate, providing the necessary administration. It does not appear Adelicia traveled there much, if at all, during the immediate period following Franklin's death.

Isaac Franklin left the majority of his considerable estate to his children, now to Emma Franklin alone. He provided handsomely for Adelicia Franklin so she and their children might live "in the best style," and it was his desire they continue to live at Fairvue. Should his widow marry again, Isaac Franklin's will directed its executors to take possession of Fairvue, and provide guardianship for the children. The will stipulated a cash payment of one hundred thousand dollars to Adelicia Franklin at her remarriage, distributed in nine installments, or through payments of six thousand dollars annually throughout her lifetime.[54] As well, Franklin's will directed a school be established on the Fairvue property, the Isaac Franklin Institute, for his children, those of his siblings, and their descendants. Franklin intended the school be funded by a percentage of the proceeds realized from the Louisiana properties, and named his brothers, James and William, as trustees. On December 1, 1847, an act passed the Tennessee legislature and incorporated the Isaac Franklin Institute.[55]

After an appropriate mourning period, and probably in 1848, Franklin attended a ball hosted by Jane Erwin Yeatman Bell, wife of John Bell, where, according to her son, William Ackland, she made the acquaintance of the tall, handsome lawyer from Huntsville, Alabama, who became her second husband, Joseph A.S. Acklen. Since Franklin's words are not available, it is helpful to include some of William's descriptions of his mother at the various stages of her life. He wrote that as she re-entered society following Isaac Franklin's death, she appeared "to bask in the silent but sumptuous haze of the soft second summer more ripe than the first," and revealed, as well, that knowledge of his mother's beauty and her wealth caused eligible bachelors from across the South to seek her out and make her acquaintance.[56]

On paper, Joseph Acklen seems a much better match for Adelicia than was Franklin. They were almost the same age, Acklen just a year Adelicia's senior, born in July of 1816; and both well educated, Acklen attended the University of Alabama before becoming a lawyer.[57] As with Franklin, a paragraph or two on Acklen's beginnings, and life prior to Adelicia Franklin, is important here, as the steps he took, and choices he made certainly influenced the direction and events of her life. Joseph Acklen's pioneer roots were as deep as Adelicia's; his forebears travelled from North Carolina in the 1790s, as had some of hers, first into Tennessee, then south to Alabama. John Hunt, the founder of Huntsville, Alabama, was Joseph Acklen's maternal grandfather; Hunt's daughter, Elizabeth, her husband, Samuel Black Acklin, and their oldest children, joined Hunt in the settlement later to bear his name in 1807, several years before Joseph Acklen's birth.[58] Samuel Black Acklin died in 1826, when Joseph was just ten years of age, and it seems he turned to his brother, William, Joseph's senior by fourteen years, for guidance and direction, and eventually followed him into the legal profession.[59] Biographical sketches of Joseph Acklen often erroneously identify him as a soldier in the Mexican-American War, fought between 1846 and 1848. His brother, C.B. "Kit" Acklin, did serve as a Texas Ranger in this war,[60] which may explain the misidentification. Joseph Acklen served in the American Southwest a decade earlier, in 1835–36 during the Texas Revolt, and with a company raised initially in Huntsville by Captain Peyton Sterling Wyatt.[61] A twenty-year-old Joseph Acklen, his university studies recently complete, might easily have been caught up in the excitement of aiding Texas gain its independence from Mexico, as were so many others, particularly across the American South. Wyatt's Company reached Texas in December of 1835, and General Sam Houston himself mustered them into the Army of the Republic of Texas. Wyatt's Company relieved another at Goliad in early January of 1836, and then in February Wyatt returned to the United States to recruit additional troops, a handful of his men accompanying him.[62] It is likely Joseph Acklen numbered among these, for on March 19, 1835, the Texas forces at Goliad surrendered to their Mexican foes, and on March 27, more than four hundred were executed under General Antonio Lopez de Santa Anna's order of "no quarter." Had Acklen remained at Goliad it is almost certain he would have numbered among the slain, and the next chapter of Adelicia's life altered significantly.[63] Instead, he settled into his law practice, and served as U.S. District Attorney for Northern and Middle Districts of Alabama from January of 1840 until his resignation in 1849, necessitated by his upcoming marriage and relocation to Nashville.[64]

Adelicia Hayes Franklin's wealth, and particularly that of her daughter, Emma Franklin, caused her to exercise caution before agreeing to marry Joseph Acklen. And while the details of both the proposal and wedding are unknown, the prenuptial agreement, without which the marriage would not take place, does survive.

Adelicia Acklen spent her Louisiana winters divided between the Angola plantation and the St. Charles Hotel in New Orleans. The original hotel burned in 1851, but in 1852 an equally grand building took its place. (Ca. 1869, Library of Congress)

Keeping in mind the year was 1849, and the legal rights of married women to their property few, the document executed by Adelicia Franklin and Joseph Acklen transferred ownership of all the real and personal property she intended to bring into the marriage to her father, Oliver B. Hayes, with the stipulation said property would be used by and for the support of Franklin and her heirs, specifically.[65] The marriage contract in place, just two months short of the tenth anniversary of her marriage to Isaac Franklin, on May 8, 1849, Adelicia Hayes Franklin and Joseph A.S. Acklen were married in a ceremony, once again, solemnized by the Reverend J.T. Edgar.[66]

Shortly after she married Acklen, Adelicia challenged Isaac Franklin's will, and the manner in which it distributed his wealth. The Louisiana Supreme Court found in her favor with its decision that the provisions of the will dealing with the establishment of the Isaac Franklin Institute were "void on the ground that it set up a perpetuity,"[67] the school he intended to create never came to fruition, and the balance of the estate reverted back to Emma and Adelicia.

Between 1850 and 1859, Adelicia and Joseph Acklen welcomed six more children into the family, three boys and three girls.[68] As was the case during her first marriage, however, Adelicia suffered a great deal of sorrow where her children were concerned. As 1855 dawned, the Acklen family included ten-year-old Emma Franklin, four-year-old Joseph Acklen, and two-and-a half year old twins, Laura and Corinne Acklen, named for Adelicia's younger sisters. In late January, while the family was in residence at its Angola plantation in Louisiana, the twins became ill with scarlet fever and died within days of each other, as had their half-sisters a decade earlier, Laura on January 25 and Corinne on February 11.[69] Illness, and particularly it seems when they were on the Louisiana plantations, was a recurring theme in family letters that do survive for, just a year prior to the twins' passing, Acklen's brother Henry Martyn Hayes—"Hal" to the family—wrote to his father he "was sorry to learn that Sister Ade's family had suffered so much by sickness—that little Buddie [Joseph H. Acklen] was reduced to a mere shadow of his former self."[70] With the loss of the twins, Acklen certainly held Emma and Joseph more closely, and both feared and anticipated the next birth; a son, William, was born in September. The year 1855 was not yet finished with Acklen, and tested her strength, determination, and faith one more time in late October when Emma became ill, and died at Belmont on November 1. "Little Emma is no more!" her grandfather, Oliver B. Hayes, wrote his son and her uncle, O.B. Hayes, Jr., on November 3, 1855, "She died night before last. The funeral will take place in Sumner Cty [County] at the vault at 4 °Clock PM of tomorrow."[71] The vault to which Hayes refers was the Fairvue vault, where Emma was interred with her father, infant brother, two sisters, and probably at this point in time, her twin half-sisters. In his introduction to "Scion of Belmont," John W. Kiser suggests William "was not so robust as his older brother Joseph and may have been overly protected by his mother."[72] Considering the trials and tribulations Adelicia Acklen was called upon to endure in 1855, it makes perfect sense she would cling to the child born amidst all of her anguish and loss.

Acklen's voice is finally heard in letters from the late 1850s, as she entered her forties, thanks to the "collecting" nature of some of her friends and relations, and particularly her sister Corinne Hayes Lawrence. Despite an age difference of almost twenty years, Adelicia and Corinne were very close and seemed to spend a significant amount of time together either at Belmont or the Lawrence home, Hillside, located just adjacent. During the winters, though, with the Acklens in Louisiana, the sisters relied on letters to keep current on the happenings in each other's lives. Acklen's surviving letters from this period deal largely with three topics: plans for upcoming trips to New Orleans or Tennessee; the health and well-being of the children—both Lawrence's and hers; and the scarcity of letters she received, particularly from family members. In and among the routine, though, are bits and pieces of information that help bring the Acklens' lives in Louisiana more clearly into focus. In February of 1857, for instance,

Acklen wrote from the St. Charles Hotel in New Orleans of the goings-on that winter season. The St. Charles was the Acklens' favorite lodging place in New Orleans, and the guest register confirms their visits to the city and the hotel—for business and pleasure—were frequent.[73] In this letter, Acklen also revealed, "Mr A seems better contented away from the plantation now he has such an excellent Agent."[74] Joseph Acklen had proved a very talented plantation manager since taking on the responsibility at their marriage, and increased both the family's holdings in Louisiana, and their productivity, but at a personal cost. In order to realize these economic successes, Acklen spent the majority of his time at the plantations, so much so, that in recalling his relationship with his father, William Acklen wrote, "My recollections of my father are vague…. Duty compelled him to look after the welfare of his dependents and he was desirous of showing the world the better side of slavery in an ideal plantation life."[75] Acklen refers here to his father's "Rules in the Management of a Southern Estate," which caught the attention of the larger planter society, and was published at least in part in the very popular *DeBow's Review*.[76]

By November of 1857, Adelicia Acklen had spent the summer in Tennessee and was once again in Louisiana, and wrote Lawrence, "I am now getting to feel settled again, and things moving on in the usual way."[77] The Acklen plantations were located some distance from the nearest towns, Bayou Sara and St. Francisville,[78] and while both Isaac Franklin and Joseph Acklen frequently attended to business matters in Bayou Sara, it does not appear Adelicia visited either town very often, if at all. Their Angola Landing, however, saw a great deal of traffic and brought the Acklens not only welcomed company, but news and information as well. "The steamer James Johnson will stop here every trip," Adelicia wrote in this same November letter, "so if you have at any time a letter ready or any especial message, it will be a grand opportunity *provided she ever gets to Nashville*,"[79] referring here to the frequent fires and accidents that plagued steamships—and steamship travel.

In late 1858, Acklen suffered yet another significant loss with the death of her father, Oliver B. Hayes.[80] After a long and prosperous life of seventy-five years, an ordained minister in his later years, Hayes died quietly at Rokeby. Hal Hayes communicated the news to his brother, Oliver, Jr., at home in Williamson County, Tennessee, and perhaps sent a similar message to Adelicia at Angola. "It is my painful duty to communicate the sad intelligence that our dear father is dead—he has just departed this life apparently with little suffering,"[81] he wrote. Personal letters and communication between Acklen and her father have not survived, but in what appeared a very close and loving relationship, Hayes's death must have struck her particularly hard. It seems Acklen learned her business savvy and acumen, displayed during the Civil War and forward, from her father. He acted as her advisor, represented her interests and

Emma's in managing and administering Franklin's estate, assisted in her eventual challenge of Franklin's will, and the two likely engaged in many conversations concerning the business and financial health of Adelicia Franklin Acklen's properties and holdings over the years. She faced the Christmas following his death without the gaiety and merriment typical of the season, and wrote Lawrence, "another '*Christmas*' has been 'buried in the past'... we passed the day very quietly... which was more in accordance with my feelings—for sad reflections would come up."[82]

Reading between the lines is the only avenue available to appreciate and understand this father-daughter bond—the strain Acklen felt in her relationship with her mother, however, is apparent, and clearly revealed in letters to Lawrence. "I should think Ma might *find time* now to write," Acklen wrote from Angola in November of 1857, a year before her father passed, "no one but her & Pa at home."[83] And in February of 1859, on receiving news her mother had canceled a planned visit to Louisiana, Acklen wrote, "that 'disappointment sinks the heart' is true—and to add to others is the intelligence that Ma had altogether given out the idea of coming down, as she promised—and too, without any excuse... But I suppose she is happier with those she thinks more of, & feels most interest in, and I should not wish it."[84] These suggestions that Sarah Hightower Hayes preferred the company of her younger daughters Laura and Corinne to Adelicia's are made in many of the surviving letters, and point to what was likely a life-long tension between these two strong-willed women.

Although raised in an urban environment, Adelicia Acklen, and the Acklens generally, seemed to truly enjoy the relative tranquility of rural life in Louisiana. "We found we had a most beautiful day & bright sun to welcome us,"[85] she wrote Lawrence in November of 1857, upon returning to the Angola plantation following a trip to New Orleans; and in February of 1858 reported, "some of the peach trees have a few flowers on them, plenty of flowers in bloom I often wish you had some of them."[86] The Acklen property was bordered on the west and south, at Tunica Bend, by the Mississippi River, located just a short distance from the Mississippi state border to the north, in sight of the Tunica Hills to the east, and included, eventually, six unique plantations: Bellevue, Lake Killarney, Lochlomond, Angola, Loango, and Panola.[87] In addition to the beauty of the landscape, as Acklen described it, the expansive holdings, totaling just about ten thousand acres, provided the Acklen children with plenty of opportunities for adventure. "Bud says he must write to Uncle Willie to tell him about his & Willies beautiful little *Welch ponies*,"[88] Acklen wrote in February of 1858; "Uncle Willie" was Corinne's husband, William L.B. Lawrence. The Acklens' third son, Claude, is first mentioned in a letter to Lawrence, probably from spring of 1858 when he was about eight months old; "little 'Claude' grows more interesting every day,"

Acklen wrote, and then noted "Willie & I were setting out some little *Cedars* yesterday."[89] William was about three years old and the picture Acklen paints of time spent with her toddler son, planting seedlings around their Louisiana home, is an important one for she is often stereotypically cast as a wealthy, elite "Southern belle;" one who certainly had no time for her children. Acklen's warmth and compassion for children is also apparent in her discussions of her husband's niece, Sallie Acklen. "Sallie & Bud went fishing yesterday & brought home quite a nice string for supper,"[90] she wrote Lawrence in March of 1859. Sallie was the daughter of Joseph's brother, John R.H. Acklen, who died in 1846. At the death of his wife, Mary, in 1859, an orphaned Sallie came to live with Joseph and Adelicia; she was probably in her mid-to-late teens at the time.[91] Sallie not only proved a good fishing partner for her young cousin, Bud, but a fine traveling companion for Adelicia, who wrote Lawrence following a trip to New Orleans in February of 1859, "Sallie was thought to be the prettiest girl at the 'St Charles.'"[92] Acklen clearly enjoyed introducing her niece to New Orleans society.

While these letters provide a welcome glimpse into the Acklens' life on the plantations, this one, in particular, reveals a bit more about Acklen herself, and her faith: "As I have been sitting sometime in the door of my room, enjoying the fresh invigorating breeze, as it is wafted by;" she wrote Lawrence in April of 1860, and looking out upon nature; now made so lovely, by the hand of God, I thought *how much* is provided for us by *his* goodness—*so many sources of enjoyment*, and how thankful we should be, and even if afflictions come, know that they are at the hand of God—and that we should not expect to have all the blessings of life, and none of its trials,—it would make this world, too delightful a dwelling place.[93]

The Acklens, as had the Franklins, left the heat and humidity of summertime Louisiana and spent those months in the cooler, and healthier, Tennessee. Adelicia Acklen had purchased a home in Nashville in 1847, much closer to Rokeby and the rest of the Hayes family than far-off Sumner County, and also sold her interest in Fairvue to Isaac Franklin's brother, William, a trustee of the academy Isaac established in his will. She continued to purchase parcels of property in Nashville in the late 1840s, most of them adjacent to Rokeby, and on one of these she and Joseph Acklen built the magnificent Belmont.[94] Perched on a hill to survey the landscape, the house contained close to thirty rooms, Venetian glass, Carrara marble fireplaces, Corinthian columns, and was thought the most magnificent home in the antebellum South.[95] "It was my mother's custom to give a large ball once a year," William Ackland recalled:

The house was lighted from attic to cellar and the rooms profusely decorated

Shortly after her marriage to Joseph A.S. Acklen in 1849, Adelicia Acklen challenged Isaac Franklin's will in the Louisiana courts. She was awarded the estate, including the cotton plantations of Panola, Belle View, Killarney, and Angola. (Detail from "Norman's Chart of the Lower Mississippi River," 1858, Library of Congress)

with flowers from the conservatories. The shrubbery on the lawn was festooned with innumerable Japanese lanterns. The lights among the trees and the bands of music on the portico were to my childish eye like a fairyland.

As magical as was Belmont, every inch decorated for these special occasions, it is clear Acklen was the shining star—to William, and perhaps others as well. "In memory I often see my mother in her beautiful gowns which came from Paris,... and seated at the piano," he wrote, "her slender fingers gracefully travelling over the keyboard in a minuet by Boccherini."[96]

William and his siblings would have observed the balls and social events, with their elegant mother at the center, from the top of Belmont's grand staircase, perhaps making an appearance for introductions before bedtime. During the day, they had the run of the estate and a multitude of amusements and activities to occupy their time. As Ackland remembered, "there was a bowling alley, billiard room, and horses and carriage were always at command. I had a Shetland pony as my own, not much larger than a big Newfoundland dog. The gates at Belmont were never closed and visitors were always welcome."[97] Those visitors often stayed days, or even weeks, and entertainment was provided for all—regardless of age. "I recall my special delight in the children's afternoon parties," William wrote, of the parties hosted not only for those in residence at Belmont, but for children from neighboring properties as well.[98]

Life was not all fun and games for the Acklen children, however, and Adelicia Acklen, for whom education was an integral part of childhood and adolescence, worked to instill a desire for knowledge, and an appreciation for learning, in her children. Ackland recalled "everybody [was to] be present at breakfast, and to break up the formality of that meal each person was asked to volunteer some scientific or historical fact.... [which] offered thought for conversation during the meal."[99] His mother clearly intended mealtime conversation to extend beyond idle chit chat.

The ebbs and flows of family life for the Acklens—the summers in Nashville and winters in Louisiana—the steamship rides to and from—the weeks-long New Orleans visits—all came to an abrupt halt when the Civil War, begun in April of 1861 with the Confederate firing on Fort Sumter in South Carolina, moved west into Kentucky and Tennessee. "They say private citizens will not be interrupted on their property,"[100] Acklen wrote from Belmont to her brother Oliver Hayes, Jr., in neighboring Williamson County, on February 16, 1862, after Forts Henry and Donelson, located on Tennessee's northern border, fell to Union forces.[101]

Based on the handful of her surviving wartime letters, Acklen did not fear the approaching federal troops; rather, it seems she carefully considered the situation, and began formulating a plan to deal with both

Union occupation and the war as it established itself in Tennessee. Laura F. Edwards has written that southern women who displayed a staunch commitment to secession were not particularly numerous, and greater numbers of them were "reluctant supporters and outright opponents of the Confederate cause."[102] Acklen falls in line here, for her letters do not reveal the zealousness associated with the proto-typical "Scarlett O'Haras" to whom she is often compared. LeeAnn Whites and Alecia P. Long have suggested, "women in occupied areas during the Civil War... were occupied, as in busy and responsive, in the face of an occupying presence,"[103] and this certainly describes Acklen and her actions.

"I thought it best to remain but prevailed upon Mr Acklen to go South," Acklen's February 16 letter to her brother continued, "he left this evening—and says you... must look after us when you can as I would have him go." It appears the Acklens' rationale here was two-fold: first, movement of Union troops into the South left harvested, but unshipped, cotton in Louisiana in danger of confiscation or destruction, and demanded Joseph Acklen's presence on site to stave off the worst;[104] and second, Acklen's public commitment to the Confederacy, evidenced by his support and funding of the "Acklen Rifles," or Company F of the Thirty-fourth Tennessee Infantry,[105] made his presence in occupied Nashville problematic—"I would be safer here without him," the letter continued.[106] As Tennessee's governor surrendered Nashville to Union troops, and the retreating Confederate army destroyed arms, bridges, and anything else of a military design as it fled,[107] Adelicia Acklen sought to protect her home, family, and personal property. Her brother Oliver lived just twelve or so miles south of Nashville on the Franklin Pike, but far enough away that items stored there might be safe, at least for the short term. "I thought it best to send one of the Carriages & pr of Horses a little further out of reach," she wrote, "and will be much obliged if you will take charge of them."[108] All indications suggest he did as she asked.

The Union army used passes and permits for civilian movement and censorship of the mail to control Nashville's population during occupation, as Acklen revealed in a number of her letters. "I enclose your Pass & permit," she wrote Oliver Hayes, in July of 1862. "I looked for Hal every day last week" she added, "his pass was for TEN days—and we all thought very strange he did not come down," referring to their brother, Henry Hayes. Acklen did secure these passes for her brothers, but such was not always the case, and as she relayed to Oliver, passes for members of his wife's family could not be obtained "without difficulty."[109] When the Union began to censor letters and randomly inspect shipments for items it considered contraband or subversive, Acklen's brothers, rather than servants or messengers, made deliveries and moved goods between households. "I reserved papers each day to send you by him [Hal]," Acklen's letter continued, "I was afraid to send them when Jim[110]

Acklen remained in Nashville at the outbreak of the Civil War, although in early 1864 she went to Louisiana to rescue her cotton. During her absence, U.S. General Thomas J. Wood appropriated Belmont and quartered his troops on the lawn. (Belmont, ca. 1864, Belmont Mansion Association)

went for fear the Inspector might object to them and then might take the other things I wanted to send I mean your Sugar & buckwheat."[111] She reveals much about Nashville under Union control here, for while occupation shut down the city's Confederate press, newspapers printed elsewhere in support of the southern cause made their way into the city, and were shared amongst the citizenry, as Acklen did here. The exchange of particular products is also telling of conditions in occupied Nashville; as Acklen provided products—the aforementioned sugar and buckwheat—to her brother in exchange for chickens, apples, and other products, in short supply in the city.[112]

By October 1862, Acklen reported "the screws tighten every day," as Union officials heightened their efforts to wrest loyalty oaths from the Nashville citizenry and "reconstruct" and restore Nashville—and Tennessee—to the Union. The crackdown on Confederate sympathizers became personal when Acklen informed Oliver Hayes that Hal "has tried every way to get off without [illeg.] the 'parole,'" and "they are obstinate at 'headquarters.'" There is no known record of Hal Hayes's arrest in 1862, but he may have been detained, and his movements restricted, at the whim of the occupying government, as was common.[113] "We go in every day to see Hal," her letter continued, "he & George keep '*batchelors' hall*.'" George Shields was Acklen's brother-in-law, the husband of her sister, Laura, and according to her letter, his movements in and out of Nashville were restricted at this time as well. "Hal says don't come down now," Acklen advised Oliver, "be careful," fearful of the acts of violence committed against Nashvillians by Union soldiers as the tension of occupation increased

In July of 1863, Acklen wrote Oliver, "We are all *loyal*."[114] Her statement, and the length of time between this letter and those from the fall of 1862, raises many questions; key among them, "loyal" to whom? Acklen had suffered no significant damage or loss to her personal property to this point in the war, but male family members were harassed and detained at times by the occupying government, and her dedication to the Confederacy did not appear to run particularly strong. In carrying out her plan to survive occupation—and survive it well—taking the oath of loyalty to the Union makes perfect sense. The mystery lies in the "if" and the true meaning behind her statement to Hayes, as no record of Acklen taking the oath at this time survives.

This is the last of Adelicia Acklen's surviving letters from the period of Union occupation, though her personal experiences continued in dramatic form until war's end. In a letter received from the Louisiana plantations dated August 20, 1863, dictated to another and signed in a very unsteady hand, Joseph Acklen revealed to Adelicia the family's precarious economic situation: "I have nothing left now but my cotton and it is uncertain if I shall be permitted to dispose of it," he wrote. "I am in constant dread of its being burned my mules and horses have all been taken and stole by the Confederates and my neighbours the places are all in ruins the crops and all waisted and waisting my only chance of support is to sell my cotton."[115] Adelicia's response to Joseph's letter is lost to history, and even if she posted one, he never received or read it. By September, Joseph Acklen was dead, malaria the most likely cause, and full responsibility for the Louisiana and Tennessee properties, and the well-being of the over eight hundred individuals living on them, fell to Adelicia. With her husband's dying words ringing in her ears, Acklen, a forty-six year old, twice-widowed, mother of four surviving children, made the decision to travel to Louisiana in wartime, negotiate with the military authorities, regardless of allegiance or color of uniform, and find a way to deliver her cotton to market.[116]

Acklen left no personal account of the cotton rescue, save a few letters housed in a thin Metro Nashville Archives file of related documents written several months after the cotton left New Orleans, so this episode, like many others in her life, must be pieced together through the documents that do exist, and the reminiscences of others. Sarah Ewing Carter (later Gaut), a neighbor and distant cousin, and Acklen's travel companion on the "cotton rescue," first reported the story to a public audience in 1902, forty years after the rescue itself, and fifteen years after Acklen's death in 1887, as part of a profile featured in Annie Somers Gilchrist's *Some Representative Women of Tennessee*.[117] Gaut penned her own piece for the September 1904 issue of the *Confederate Veteran*, at a time, according to Catherine Clinton, experiencing "an explosion of interest in Southern plantation lore."[118]

As the story goes, upon news of Joseph Acklen's death, the perilous circumstances concerning their cotton, and her dire financial situation, Adelicia Acklen enlisted the company Gaut and the two traveled—possibly with a male escort, perhaps without—from Nashville to Louisiana's West Feliciana Parish to somehow bring about release of the cotton. "She [Acklen] insisted on my going down with her," Gaut wrote in the 1904 article, "thinking she could sell the cotton in New Orleans," adding this "would have been impossible, as it was in Confederate lines and being watched." Gaut reported she traveled "one hundred and fifty miles eight times, in the Confederate lines, to Jackson and Clinton, La., and finally got permission for her [Acklen] to ship the cotton to Europe." All the while, Acklen apparently remained at her plantations, sidelined by illness or malady. "We got... a permit to take it [the cotton] to New Orleans, and she [Acklen] realized nine hundred and sixty thousand dollars. It was a tremendous undertaking." The back story revolves around an order issued by Confederate General Leonidas Polk instructing plantation owners and managers in the Red River region to burn any cotton on hand to prevent its capture by the Union Army. This order, as expected, was objected to, and generally ignored, by growers hoping to someday profit from the cotton. "Through the intercession of Col. Dillon... I secured the General's permission for Mrs. Acklin to store her cotton 'at some safe place on the river' until it could be exported,"[119] Gaut concluded, and thus was born the story of Adelicia Acklen and the Great Cotton Rescue of 1864.

It does appear Gaut served as Acklen's "legs" and messenger in this endeavor, but Acklen clearly conducted negotiations for release and transport of the cotton herself, as evidenced in correspondence directed, and referring, to her and it by members of both armies. A letter from Confederate Lieutenant and Assistant Adjutant General Joseph C. Robert, dated January 31, 1864,

In early 1864, Adelicia Acklen enlisted the help of her cousin Sarah Carter to rescue the Acklens' cotton in Louisiana. The women convinced both Confederate and Union officers to help them. Several hundred bales made it to Liverpool for sale. (Sarah Ewing Carter, Belmont Mansion Association)

clarified the burning order and advised Acklen that Colonel Dillon's "intention is not to burn the cotton until it is in imminent danger of being taken by the enemy."[120] Events moved quickly, and by late March, Acklen's cotton was no longer in danger of being burned by the Confederates, but under their protection, according to an order attributed to General Polk himself, a fellow Tennessean and close Acklen family friend, which stated, "a safe guard is hereby granted to the cotton of Mrs Acklen which lies on or near the Mississippi River. All Confederate officers & men are hereby ordered to respect the same."[121] Within days, authorization issued from the Headquarters of Southwest Mississippi and Eastern Louisiana at Camp Dick Garnett stated, "in anticipation of authority to sell her cotton to foreigners (under a guarantee of protection by the Confederate Authorities) Mrs Ada Acklen of Angola Plantation is authorized move her cotton (two thousand bales or more) to some point on the Miss River, there to remain unmolested by any Confederate Officer or soldier."[122]

In mid-April, less than three months after Acklen's first communication, and likely negotiation, with the Confederate Army, the first five hundred and eighty bales of Acklen cotton left Confederate protection and shipped to New Orleans for delivery to Acklen's cotton agents, per an order approved by the ship's commanding officer, Acting Volunteer Lieutenant Cyrenius Dorning, U.S.N.[123] How Acklen managed this transfer of cotton from one army to the other remains uncertain. It is apparent, however, that a great deal of confusion surrounded the Acklen cotton matter. Two days after Lieutenant Dorning's confirmation of shipment, Lieutenant Roberts wrote Colonel Frank Powers, commanding the Fourteenth Arkansas Infantry and on duty near the Acklen property: "The Genl [Gen. Thomas H. Taylor] is considerably surprised at that part of your letter of the 14th inst which relates to Capt Cammack shipping Mrs Acklen's cotton. No such authority has been given him by me."[124] The captain, most likely Captain R.C. Cammack of the First Louisiana Artillery,[125] oversaw the transfer of Acklen's cotton, and armed with the various orders previously referenced here, for all intents and purposes, at least to the casual observer, he simply carried out orders. The response by Brigadier General Taylor, adds to the confusion. Did Cammack receive some sort of monetary enticement from Acklen to release the cotton for transport, or was he taken in by fraudulent orders? Were the "no-burn" and authorization for transport orders properly issued by Generals Polk and Taylor, or was there impropriety there? A July 1864 report from George Hodge, Assistant Inspector General to Confederate President Jefferson Davis gives a bit of credence, albeit just a bit, to the latter. In his report concerning "the abuses alleged to have characterized the administration of military affairs" in several Louisiana and Mississippi counties, including West Feliciana, General Hodge commented on the shipment of Acklen cotton and remarked, "the details of the transaction point with… unpleasant suggestiveness to officers at one time high in command in this district."[126] It is difficult to argue with the prevailing school of thought that Acklen received Confederate assistance—authorized or not—in the release of her cotton.

Nashville Civil War stories and legends suggest Acklen also made deals with the Union army, though evidence shows those accusations may be unfounded. On May 13, 1864, Lieutenant Commander K.R. Breese, U.S.N., issued a notification to Union ships in the Red River region of his authorization allowing shipment of twenty-eight bales of cotton and six hundred bags of cotton in seed from the Acklen plantations to New Orleans. Within the document is a single line that makes complete sense of the Union navy's role in the cotton rescue. "She [Acklen] has taken the Amnesty Oath," Breese noted.[127] With the oath, and Acklen's stated loyalty to the Union, the United States Navy found no irregularity in transporting the Acklen cotton to New Orleans for eventual shipment and sale in Britain.

The cotton rescue accomplished, Acklen and Gaut traveled from New Orleans to New York aboard the steamer *Evening Star*,[128] and returned to Middle Tennessee in mid-1864, in time to witness the Battle of Nashville. William Ackland remembered that on his mother's return to Belmont, she found Union General Thomas J. Wood had appropriated her Nashville home as his headquarters, and quartered his troops on its lawns. "We drove out daily from the city to Belmont and it was distressing to see the country denuded of trees and the magnificent forests around Belmont felled to furnish necessary firewood to the Federal soldiers," he recalled. Concerned soldiers having the run of Belmont would result in extensive damage to her possessions, Acklen removed much of her artwork, silver, and other valuables to the home of Sarah Childress Polk, widow of former President James K. Polk, for safe keeping. On December 15, 1864, the Battle of Nashville played out between Wood's Union soldiers and John Bell Hood's Confederate army on the Belmont property and countless others throughout the city. Nashville lore suggests Acklen and the children watched and listened to the battle from the relative safety of Polk Place, though in Ackland's reminiscence he reported he "saw from the roof of Belmont the Battle of Nashville in the distance."[129] In either case, for Acklen the night was likely long and sleepless, filled with dread of the condition in which she might find her beloved Belmont in the morning. Amazingly, the house survived unscathed, and as December 16 dawned, Hood's army retreated from Nashville with Wood's in pursuit,[130] and Nashville fell back into its now strangely-familiar state of occupation.

Four months later the war was effectively over, and within weeks of Robert E. Lee's April, 1865, surrender to U.S. Grant at Appomattox, Acklen packed up her four children, and perhaps some of the family's servants, and sailed out of New York for an extended tour of Europe. Some accounts of Acklen's life suggest she had travelled abroad on other occasions, in particular at the time of her marriage to Joseph Acklen in 1849, but it is clear from a letter written to her mother from Newport, upon her return to the U.S. in the summer of 1866, that this trip was her first across the Atlantic. "I have had (more especially when young) an ardent desire to visit Europe, and see something of the world on the other side of the great Ocean," she wrote. "Now that wish is gratified and I hope too to the benefit of my children."[131] Just a few of the letters Acklen wrote during the year she and the children spent away from the South survive, but those are rich in detail and description and not only provide a look at international travel in the nineteenth century, but Acklen's reactions to sights and sounds with which she was unfamiliar. "It is just four weeks today since we sailed from N York," she wrote her mother on July 28, 1865, from London's Langham Hotel, "I visited the *Tunnel* under the Thames yesterday & walked entirely through & back descending & ascending one hundred steps... It is considered one of the great curiosities here."[132] Each letter contained news of the children and their activities, governesses engaged, schools attended, and the like. Considering the young ages of her children[133] makes Adelicia's undertaking even more remarkable—even with the aid of servants—and lends understanding to her need, though she never discussed it, to put distance between herself and the U.S. South, at least for a time.

In September of 1865, the *New York Herald* reported, "American visitors who registered in Paris for the week ending August 10" included "Mrs. A. Acklen and family, Miss Acklen, Nashville."[134] It appears the family's stay in Paris was a lengthy one, lasting the entire fall and through the New Year, and necessitated enrolling Joseph in school and engaging tutors for the younger children. "Their delight," Acklen wrote her mother, "is to go to the 'Champs Elysees' where they meet so many little children.... It is a pleasure to take a promenade on the streets here... This is the nicest city I suppose in the world."[135] Acklen often shunned large gatherings at home in the United States—unless she was the host—and in many letters written from New Orleans over the years she recounts the operas and balls she opted not to attend, for one reason or another. In the France of Napoleon III, however, such invitations were not declined, and, as the newspapers reported in the winter of 1866: "At Napoleon's last court ball twenty-four American ladies and gentlemen were presented," among them, "Mrs. Acklen and daughter, of Tennessee."[136]

A recurring topic in Acklen's letters from Europe was the plentitude of flowers to be found in almost every European city: "I have been enjoying the sweet flowers here so much," she wrote from Rome in February of 1866, and was particularly taken by the gift, "by a *Roman*" of "the most exquisite Camelias and a variety of other flowers that would fill a half bushel." Rome itself did not impress Acklen as had Paris, she found it "not at all a handsome City and a very *dirty* one too," but she was taken by the culture and history, and wrote her mother, "I have been more interested here than at any place I have been except Paris… here it is of a different Character—The old Ruins the Palaces, Temples, Arches… are historical." More than seven months had passed since Acklen and her little entourage departed the United States, and it seems, at last, she missed home: "I have heard so much of the bright skies of Italy and gorgeous sun sets—I do not find them more bright than our own nor have I seen a sun-set to equal many I have witnessed at Belle Monte. I may be partial, but I think our own America the most beautiful Country after all—True we have no such city as *Paris* but I look in vain for the magnificent forests of America and beauty of natural scenery."[137]

One of the most charming pictures from this family adventure occurred during a brief stopover at Nice, France, as the Acklens made their way back toward London. "I was delighted to find myself in so mild & spring like an atmosphere with fruit trees all in full bloom and every thing so green around," Adelicia wrote. The children "were delighted standing on the beaches watching the surf and the breakers as they came crashing in to their feet forcing them to run from them," she continued, "and in picking up pebbles—Willie had his overcoat pockets filled with them."[138]

By early July, they were back in New York, spending time with extended family and projecting a return to Tennessee by late August; "I have promised Buddy he should go home and his session commences the 10th of Sept,"[139] Acklen wrote Corinne Lawrence on July 2 from the 5th Avenue Hotel. In the meantime, the family enjoyed some summer fun and relaxation at the shore in Newport, Rhode Island. "I think the sun-bathing and sea air has had a beneficial effect upon us all," Acklen wrote her mother, "the Children enjoy the bathing very much it is so entirely new to them." Newport's social goings-on during the summer season differed significantly from those she had recently experienced in Europe; "the company is still small—the Ladies dress very little, and it is very *quiet* which is much more to my taste for I do not at any time fancy crowds especially *fashionable* ones—I find the older I grow the more I shrink from fashionable society, and it becomes a bore to me."[140]

"Sis Ade has returned home—all well,"[141] Oliver B. Hayes, Jr., wrote Sallie Acklen in September of 1866, upon Adelicia Acklen's return to Nashville. Sallie did not accompany the Acklens on their European tour as during the war she fell in love with, and subsequently married, Southard Hoffman, a Union soldier, and moved with him to New York.[142] According to William Ackland, his mother resumed her position on Nashville's social ladder without delay, and in December of 1866 hosted a grand reception for visiting Alabama socialite, preservationist, and women's rights advocate, Octavia LeVert.[143] "Perhaps the profuse but refined hospitality for which the

In the summer of 1865, Acklen packed up her children for a year-long tour of Europe. While in Paris for several months, she posed for a portrait with her daughter Pauline. (Belmont Mansion Association)

South is so famous has never been more aptly illustrated," the *Republican Banner* wrote of the event, and the "pleasant memories"[144] more than five hundred invited guests carried away from it.

Adelicia Hayes Franklin Acklen married for the third and final time a year after her return from Europe, and her decision to do so is both interesting and curious. She survived the war without significant damage to any of her personal property, and with proceeds from the cotton sale safely tucked away did not "need" to re-marry. Perhaps, as her younger children were still quite young, she saw a need for a father-figure in the household. Perhaps, at age fifty, she missed the companionship of a husband. As was so often the case, Acklen did not leave behind reasons for her actions; she did, however, on June 18, 1867 at Belmont, marry Dr. William A. Cheatham, a well-known and respected medical doctor, and she did so "most gorgeously,"[145] according to the *Springfield Republican*.[146] Prior to the ceremony, a marriage contract was drawn that conveyed all of Adelicia Acklen's assets to George Shields, as trustee, but to be used and controlled by Acklen for her benefit and enjoyment, and that of her children. This document reached farther than had her marriage contract with Joseph Acklen, and with his execution of it, Cheatham renounced any interest in her assets, as well as community property interests generated by the Louisiana properties during their marriage.[147]

While Adelicia Acklen's third husband is often misidentified as "General" Cheatham of Confederate Civil War fame, William Archer Cheatham did not serve in the war, but it directly and dramatically affected him, his future, and Acklen's as well. Three years his wife's junior, Cheatham was the son of Robertson County, Tennessee's General Richard Cheatham and his wife, Kentucky-born Susan Saunders Cheatham, and earned a medical degree from the University of Pennsylvania in 1843. Cheatham married Mary Emma Ready of Murfreesboro in 1847, and the couple had two children—Martha, born in 1853 and Richard, in 1855. In 1852, Cheatham was named superintendent of the Tennessee Lunatic Asylum, recently constructed in Nashville in response to the national reform movement spearheaded by Dorothea A. Dix, who visited often and praised both Cheatham and the institution.[148] The asylum's trustees extended his term an additional eight years in 1859, but in July of 1862, Cheatham was abruptly dismissed from his position as Union occupation made itself felt in Nashville. In May of 1863, William and Mary Cheatham were arrested; the charge, corresponding with the enemy. Mary Cheatham was the sister-in-law of notorious Confederate guerrilla, John Hunt Morgan, and the Union had intercepted letters written by her to Hunt's wife and Mary's sister, Mattie. The Cheathams were ordered to the federal prison at Alton, Illinois, for the duration of the war, but on the journey north, Mary suffered what was termed a nervous breakdown, and sympathetic Union authorities allowed their return to Nashville. Her health never recovered, and in April of 1864, Mary Ready Cheatham died, leaving her husband a widower and her children, aged nine and eleven, motherless.[149]

It appears, from a surviving collection of Mattie Cheatham letters, Acklen formed strong and loving relationships with her step-children, and perhaps they represent one of the reasons for this marriage. After losing six of her children in early childhood, the Cheatham children likely tugged at Adelicia's maternal heartstrings. Their ages also closely aligned with those of the Acklens, and by all appearances all of the children accepted each other as siblings almost immediately. Acklen's letters to Mattie and Richard Cheatham contained family news from Belmont, many endearments, and were always signed by Acklen as "Mother." At the bottom of one of these, written in the fall of 1868 while she was away at boarding school, Mattie wrote, "From my beloved mother If I could only receive sweet letters every day How very very happy sweet cheering letters make me."[150]

The early years of this marriage, and the coming together of this large family, were happy times for Adelicia Acklen Cheatham. William Cheatham continued his medical practice and assisted with the management of Adelicia's vast properties, and she supervised the children, their educations, the daily management of Belmont, and engaged civically and socially in Nashville.

In the summer of 1867, she presented an enormous bell, the largest in the city, to the church she had attended all of her life, the First Presbyterian Church;[151] she kept "open house" on New Year's Day into the 1870s, despite the tradition losing some of its popularity among Nashville's gentlewomen;[152] and in the late 1870s, in conjunction with the local school board, provided for the establishment of an African-American school on the Lake Killarney plantation in Louisiana.[153] The plantations themselves, though, had created great consternation for Adelicia since Joseph Acklen's death, and it only intensified in the decade of the 1870s.

In 1865, prior to her European tour, Adelicia Acklen leased the Louisiana properties, with outbuildings, stock, supplies, and an allowance for logging on the property all included, for a period of two years, and at a price of $15,000 for the first year and $25,000 for the second.[154] On her return, with the physical effects of the Civil War still fresh and the difficulty and cost of maintaining a labor force after the introduction of the Thirteenth Amendment abolishing slavery, she renewed those leases, as evidenced by the advertisement placed in the *Nashville Union & Dispatch* by her brother-in-law and agent, George Shields, in July of 1867. "Three highly improved places situated in North Louisiana, opposite the mouth of Red River," the ad read, "will be leased on very reasonable terms this season with the privilege of three years."[155]

Acklen resumed management of the plantations through on-site managers in the late 1860s, but it was becoming clear she could no longer realize a profit from them, and for numerous reasons. Repairs and upkeep previously undertaken by enslaved laborers, and particularly attention to the levees essential to keeping Mississippi River floodwaters at bay, were not undertaken by tenant farmers and managers, and the weakening and breaching of those levees, accompanied by the arrival of the boll weevil, "made the culture of cotton so precarious that the land ceased to yield an income,"[156] as William Ackland later recalled. In late 1871, Adelicia Acklen Cheatham wrote Corinne Lawrence from Louisiana, "Joseph & I have settled our business matters without the assistance of lawyers or the Courts, which we thought was much better."[157] Those "business matters" involved Cheatham buying out her eldest son's interest in the plantations, which allowed her to "manage to suit myself." This seems to be Cheatham's last effort at making the plantations profitable; it is also the first time, at least in surviving letters, she expressed strong political views. "These Radicals are ruining the state," she wrote Lawrence in February of 1872, blaming the Radical Republican Congress, and the Reconstruction governments in place throughout the post-war South, for not only high taxes, but crop failures and foreclosures.[158]

Adelicia Cheatham made only a few references in her letters to those who labored on her properties in Tennessee and Louisiana—both during slavery and after its abolition—most of them assigning tasks to be accomplished, or reporting on births, marriages, and deaths. And while she never revealed her thoughts or opinions on slavery, she did feel responsible for the well-being of those who worked for her—some of whom she had known all of her life. In 1874, for instance, during particularly difficult economic times, Cheatham refused to lay-off laborers on the plantations, and leave them without a means of support.[159] Her daily contact and communication with her laborers increased in the 1870s, with her resumption of administrative control of the plantations, and the few surviving accounts of them are instructive in better understanding the complex relationships that existed in the Reconstruction South. "Morning brought us alongside the landing at 'Angola,'" Ackland recalled of a trip to the plantations during this time. "My mother was welcomed as if she had been a queen setting foot on her own domain," he continued, "she shook hands with the overseer and then in turn with the 'oldest settlers' as they called themselves. A certain precedence was observed as to age and residence. They followed her to the house and on the rear porch of the house those who did not meet her at the landing came 'to pay their respects.'"[160] Cheatham wrote of these relationships herself in 1875, in a letter from the plantations to Corinne Lawrence. "The old servants here seem delighted to have me here," she wrote, "and so grateful to see I still feel an interest in them."[161]

In 1880, now in her sixties, Adelicia Cheatham made the difficult decision to

In June 1867, Adelicia Acklen married her third husband, William Cheatham, a well-known and respected medical doctor. Once more Acklen insured control of her assets through a detailed pre-nuptial agreement. (Belmont Mansion Association)

divest herself and her family of most of the Louisiana property, and sold the plantations, comprising about ten thousand acres, to Samuel L. James and Louis Trager for the sum of one hundred thousand dollars, guaranteed by sixteen promissory notes, with first payments due on December 22, 1887.[162] She had previously sold the Texas properties, and sold Fairvue in 1882, but continued to accumulate real estate, purchasing lots in Orlando, Florida, and Washington, D.C.

"Mrs. Cheatham and her daughter, Miss Acklen, will see their friends after January 1st

Adelicia Acklen died in 1887 and was entombed in the Acklen vault with her first two husbands and her children. Her statue, *The Peri*, was moved from Belmont's Grand Salon to the vault. (Tennessee Historical Society)

on Wednesdays from three to five O'clock at their home, 5 Iowa Circle,"[163] the *Evening Star* reported in late December of 1885. In an interesting show of independence, or perhaps restlessness, and maybe boredom, Adelicia left her life-long Tennessee home, re-established herself in the nation's capital, and soon became a part its society circle. In doing so, though, she also left behind William Cheatham, and while the couple never divorced, Adelicia Cheatham's move renews questions as to why she opted for this marriage in the first place. Cheatham sold Belmont and its acreage in 1887, and most of her other Nashville properties, and with construction of her new Washington, D.C., home well underway, she and Pauline Acklen traveled to New York to select and purchase its furniture and finishing accessories. While there, Adelicia Cheatham developed such a severe case of pneumonia, the *Evening Star* reported "members of her family in Washington have been telegraphed to go to her."[164] After a brief rebound, her health declined rapidly, and on the evening of May 4, 1887, at the Fifth Avenue Hotel, Adelicia Hayes Franklin Acklen Cheatham died.[165] Her remains were transported to Nashville and her funeral held at the First Presbyterian Church. Construction on the Acklen vault in Mount Olivet Cemetery was completed in 1884, and there Adelicia was laid to her final rest with members of her immediate family.[166]

"I wish there had been a visitor's Book at Belmont for no celebrity who visited Nashville left Belmont unvisited,"[167] William Ackland wrote years after the sale of the home where he spent his youth. A visitor's book, a diary or two, a more extensive collection of letters—the things of which historians and researchers dream—any of these would help develop the picture of the woman sketched in this essay. With the information provided here though, as spotty as it is, that image begins to come into clearer focus. Adelicia Acklen was an elite, wealthy, white woman living in the antebellum South, to those points there is no argument. But she was also a wife, a mother, a daughter, and a sister who loved her family, celebrated their joys, and suffered their sorrows. She was an astute businesswoman who understood the well-being of hundreds of individuals depended on her, at wartime and in peace, and was determined to provide it. And she was a patroness of the city she loved, although she was often unappreciated and misunderstood by many of its citizens. Adelicia Acklen, as revealed here, is an ideal example of nineteenth-century Southern white womanhood. She should be appreciated for the contributions she made to the history of Nashville and the South, and remembered for far more than the big pink house on the hill.

1. Anita Shafer Goodstein, *Nashville, 1780–1860: From Frontier to City*, Gainesville: University of Florida Press, 1989, 24.

2. "Williamson County Genealogy and History," www.genealogytrails.com/tenn/williamson/history/goodspeeds.html, accessed February 23, 2011.

3. "Yesterday Nashville," *The Nashville American*, August 15, 1909.

4. Ancestry.com. *Tennessee State Marriages, 1780–2002* [database on-line}, accessed July 16, 2016.

5. Numerous sources discuss the establishment of Nashville and its environs, among them are: Alfred Leland Crabb, *Nashville: Personality of a City* (Indianapolis: The Bobbs-Merrill Co., Inc., 1960); Goodstein, *Nashville, 1780–1860: From Frontier to City*; Nashville-Gallatin Interurban Railway, *The Historic Blue Grass Line: A Review of the History of Davidson and Sumner Counties, together with Sketches of Places and Events along the Route of the Nashville-Gallatin Interurban Railway* (Ann Arbor: University of Michigan, 1913); Edward Albright, *Early History of Middle Tennessee* (Nashville: Brandon Printing Company, 1909); Charles E. Robert, *Nashville and Her Trade for 1870* (Nashville: Roberts & Purvis, 1870); A.W. Putnam, Esq., *History of Middle Tennessee; or, Life and Times of Gen. James Robertson* (Nashville: Southern Methodist Publishing House, 1859); Paul H. Bergeron, Stephen V. Ash, and Jeanette Keith, *Tennesseans and Their History* (Knoxville: University of Tennessee Press, 1999);

and Robert E. Corlew, *Tennessee. A Short History* 2d (Knoxville: University of Tennessee Press, 1993.)

6. Kristofer Ray, *Middle Tennessee, 1775–1825. Progress and Popular Democracy on the Southwestern Frontier* (Knoxville: University of Tennessee Press, 2007), 60.

7. Ray, *Middle Tennessee 1775–1825*, 58.

8 Ibid, 75.

9. L. Cheves to F. Grundy, J. Whiteside, and O.B. Hayes, June 16, 1819, U.S. Congress, *Congressional Edition*, Washington, D.C.: Government Printing Office, 1834): 238.

10. John Roderick Heller, *Democracy's Lawyer: Felix Grundy of the Old Southwest* (Baton Rouge, Louisiana State University Press, 2010), 116; *Nashville Whig*, 20 December 1820; William J. Tenney, ed., *Mining Magazine devoted to Mines, Mining Operations, Metallurgy, &c, &c*, vol. 4, New York: John F. Trow, 1855, 273; *Nashville Republican*, 23 August 1836; *1690–1940: 250 Years of Papermaking in America*, New York: Lockwood Trade Journal Co., 1940, 17.

11. www.grandlodge-tn.org/index/php?past_grand_officers=Y&record_key=000970&page=BL. Accessed June 19, 2012.

12. "Passing of Old Landmark to Make Room for Hotel," *Nashville Tennessean and The Nashville American*, November 17, 1912.

13. "Yester Nashville," *The Nashville American*, August 15, 1909.

14. "Passing of Old Landmark to Make Room for Hotel," *Nashville Tennessean and The Nashville American*, November 17, 1912.

15. Oliver Bliss Hayes, Jr., was born in 1825. A sister, Corinna, born in 1819, died by the age of two, and a first Oliver Bliss Hayes, Jr., born in 1821, died before his third birthday. The four youngest Hayes children were born after the family moved to its "Rokeby" estate.

16. Lee Nathaniel Newcomer, ed., "Two New England Teachers in Nashville, 1818," *Tennessee Historical Quarterly* 19:1 (March 1960): 74–5; Lucius Salisbury Merriam, Ph.D., "Higher Education in Tennessee," *Bureau of Education Circular of Information No. 5, 1893* (Washington: Government Printing Office, 1893): 245.

17. Mrs. I.M.E. Blandin, *History of Higher Education of Women in the South Prior to 1860* (New York: The Neale Publishing Co., 1909), 274–277.

18. "Founders of the Nashville Female Academy," Collins D. Elliott Papers, 1816–1932, mf. 802, Tennessee State Library and Archives (TSLA), Nashville, TN.

19. "Bill of Recitations for the Twentieth Session of the Nashville Female Academy, Commencing January 22d and ending June 21st, 1827," http://teva.contentdm.oclc.org/cdm/singleitem/collection/broadsides/id/44/rec/3, accessed July 20, 2016.

20. "List of Students, 1839," Collins D. Elliott Papers, 1816–1932, mf. 802, TSLA.

21. "Ghosts May Feel Housing Shortage When Wreckers Raze Rokeby Place," unknown newspaper, n.d.

22. "Yester Nashville," *The Nashville American*, August 15, 1909. There were, in fact, four surviving Hayes sisters, Adelicia, Laura, Aurelia, and Corinne, though no mention of Aurelia is made in any of the family's surviving records. Aurelia (1835–1850) is buried in the Richard Hightower Cemetery and, for reasons that remain unclear, may have spent the majority of her time with her maternal grandparents, Richard and Nancy Smith Hightower. http://www.findagrave.com/cgi-bin/fg.cgi?page=gr&GScid=2170529&GRid=35998175&, accessed May 21, 2013.

23. At some point during their engagement, Gibbs and Hayes had their portraits painted; those portraits remain in the Gibbs family collection. http://www.tngenweb.org/williamson/history/tsfamhisEFG.html. Accessed February 1, 2011.

24. Harvard Law School. *Quinquennial Catalogue of the Officers and Students of the Law School of Harvard University* (Cambridge: The Law School, 1900), 54.

25. *National Banner and Nashville Whig*, October 3, 1834; "Memory of the Dead," *Nashville Republican and State Gazette*, October 7, 1834.

26. Amelia Opie, *Lays for the Dead* (London: Longman, Rees, Orme, Brown, Green & Longman, 1834), 40–42.

27. Isaac Franklin began construction of Fairvue in 1832. See, Albert W. Wardin, Jr., *Belmont Mansion. The Home of Joseph and Adelicia Acklen* (Nashville: Belmont Mansion Associates, 2002), 3.

28. Eleanor Graham, "Belmont: Home of Adelicia Acklen," *Tennessee Historical Quarterly* 30:4 (1971): 349.

29. Caroline Seebohm and Peter Woloszynski, *Under Live Oaks, The Last Great Houses of the Old South* (New York: Clarkson Potter, 2002), 179.

30. As an adult, William Acklen changed the spelling of his last name to "Ackland," its English variant. See, John W. Kiser, "Scion of Belmont," Part I, *Tennessee Historical Quarterly* 38:1 (Spring 1979): 34.

31. Kiser, "Scion of Belmont," Part I 39.

32. Ancestry.com. Tennessee State Marriages, 1780–2002 [database on-line]., accessed July1, 2016; *Nashville Whig,* July 5, 1839.

33. Wendell Holmes Stephenson, *Isaac Franklin. Slave Trader and Planter of the Old South,* reprint (Gloucester, MA: Peter Smith, 1968), 19.

34. *Under the Live Oaks,* 179.

35. Albright, *Early History of Middle Tennessee,* 51. For information specific to Kasper Mansker and his expeditions, see, Walter Durham, "Kasper Mansker Cumberland Frontiersman, *Tennessee Historical Quarterly* 30:2 (1971): 154–77.

36. William Saunders, ed., "Acts of the North Carolina General Assembly, 1784," *The Colonial Records of North Carolina*, v. 24, (Raleigh: P.M. Hale, Printer to the State, 1886): 629–630; "Isaac Franklin," *Mississippi Free Trader*, October 21, 1846.

37. Stephenson, *Isaac Franklin,* 14–15.

38. Ibid, 15; "Isaac Franklin," *Mississippi Free Trader*, October 21 1846.

39. National Archives Records Administration, *Index to the Compiled Military Service Records for the Volunteer Soldiers Who Served During the War of 1812* (Washington, D.C.: National Archives and Records Administration), Roll Box 75, Roll Exct. 602. Corporal William Franklin numbered among the members of this regiment as well, more than likely the younger brother of Isaac Franklin.

40. Louisiana Supreme Court, *The Succession of Isaac Franklin*, (n.p., 1851?): 277–78, 285, 287.

41. Sumner County (Tennessee) Deed Record, VII (1814–1817), 280–81.

42. There are many good works on the rise of the domestic slave trade in the early nineteenth century. Among them: Steven Deyle, *Carry Me Back. The Domestic Slave Trade in American Life* (New York: Oxford University Press, 2005); Walter Johnson, ed., *The Chattel Principle. Internal Slave Trades in the Americas* (New Haven: Yale University Press, 2004); Robert H. Gudmestad, *A Troublesome Commerce. The Transformation of the Interstate Slave Trade* (Baton Rouge: Louisiana State University Press, 2003.)

43. Adams County (Mississippi) Deed Record, K, 491.

44. Jim Barnett and H. Clark Burkett, "The Forks of the Road Slave Market at Natchez," *The Journal of Mississippi History* 63:3 (Fall 2001): 171.

45. Wendell Holmes Stephenson, *Isaac Franklin, Slave Trader and Planter of the Old South* (Baton Rouge: LSU Press, 1938), 23–4, 55.

46. Joseph Holt Ingraham, *The Southwest by a Yankee, vol. II* (NY: Harper and Brothers, 1835) 245, Kindle edition.

47. See, in particular, Michael Tadman, "The Reputation of the Slave Trader in Southern History and the Social Memory of the South," *American Nineteenth Century History* 8:3 (September 2007): 247–271.

48. Deed between John Travason and Francis Routh, 21 December 1832, Acklen Papers, Special Collections, Howard-Tilton Memorial Library, Tulane University, New Orleans, LA; Bill of Sale, April 2, 1834, Acklen Papers, Special Collections, Howard-Tilton Memorial Library, Tulane University, New Orleans, LA; Bill of Sale, December 26, 1834, Acklen Papers, Special Collections, Howard-Tilton Memorial Library, Tulane University, New Orleans.

49. Isaac Franklin to Rice C. Ballard, May 20, 1834, Rice C. Ballard Papers, Southern Historical Collection, Louis B. Round Memorial Library, University of North Carolina, Chapel Hill.

50. Stephenson, *Isaac Franklin*, 66–67.

51. Ibid,104–105.

52. *Alexandria (VA) Gazette*, May 14, 1846.

53. *Nashville Union,* 16 June 16, 1846.

54. "Isaac Franklin's Will," in Stephenson, *Isaac Franklin*, 148.

55. Stephenson, *Isaac Franklin,* 118.

56. Kiser, "Scion of Belmont," Part I, 40.

57. Thomas Waverly Palmer, comp., *A Register of the Officers and Students of the University of Alabama, 1831–1901* (Tuscaloosa: University of Alabama, 1901), 41.

58. "The Story of John Hunt," *Old Huntsville. History and Stories of the Tennessee Valley* 215 (January 2011):30–37.

59. Thomas McAdory Owen, LL.D., *History of Alabama and Dictionary of Alabama Biography,* vol. III (Chicago: The S.J. Clarke Publishing Co., 1921), 8.

60. Darren L. Ivey, *The Texas Rangers: A Registry and History* (Jefferson, N.C.: McFarland & Co., Inc., Publishers, 2010), 67.

61. "Index to Military Rolls of the Republic of Texas, 1835–1845," www.tshaonline.org/supsites/military/n/fannjw3n.htm, accessed February 17, 2011.

62. "Peyton Sterling Wyatt," www.tshaonline.org/handbook/onlin/articles/fyw01, accessed July 2, 2013.

63. In 1859, Joseph Acklen received a donation land grant in Texas for his service during the 1836 revolt, some or all of which property he subsequently deeded to his brother, Arthur A. Acklen. www.glo.texas.gov/ncu/SCANDOCS/archives_webfiles/arc-maps/webfiles/landgrants/PDFs/3/0/1/301564.pdf, accessed July 12, 2016.

64. *Sun,* January 27, 1840; *Alexandria Gazette*, March 16, 1844; *Philadelphia Inquirer* March 27, 1848; *Daily National Intelligencer,* July 27, 1849.

65. Marriage Contract between Adelicia Franklin and Jos. A.S. Acklen, dated May 7, 1849, registered May 9, 1849, Marriage Contracts, book 12, page 214, Registrar, Davidson County, Tennessee.

66. Ancestry.com. Tennessee State Marriages, 1780–2002, accessed July 5, 2016.

67. 7 La. Ann. 395 (1852), in Stephenson, *Isaac Franklin,* 119.

68. Joseph H. Acklen, born May 20, 1850; the twins Laura and Corinne, born October 20, 1852; William H., born September 6, 1855; Claude M., born July 25, 1857; and Pauline, born October 10, 1859.

69. Wardin, *Belmont Mansion*, 7.

70. Henry M. Hayes to Oliver B. Hayes, May 21, 1854, Hayes Family Papers (HFP), 1848–1888, micro. 1169–1, Tennessee States Library and Archives, Nashville.

71. Oliver B. Hayes to O.B. Hayes, Jr., November 3, 1855, HFP, TSLA.

72. Kiser, "Scion of Belmont," Part I, 35.

73. *The Daily Picayune,* November 16, 1850; *Times Picayune,* April 10, 1852; *The Daily Picayune,* February 15, 1853; *Times-Picayune,* April 7, 1855; *New Orleans Daily Crescent,* March 17, 1859.

74. Adelicia Acklen to Corinne Lawrence, February 8, 1857, McGavock-Hayes Papers (MHP), micro. 68–6, TSLA.

75. Kiser, "Scion of Belmont, Part I, 42-3.

76. Joseph A.S. Acklen, "Rules in the Management of a Southern Estate," *DeBow's Review and Industrial Resources, Statistics, etc.* Vol. XXI–Third Series, Vol. I (Washington City, 1856), 617–620.

77. Adelicia Acklen to Corinne Lawrence, November 28, 1857, MHP, TSLA.

78. Bayou Sara was located on the Mississippi River, St. Francisville on the bluffs above, and though in close physical proximity, the two developed very differently and perhaps were best described by newspaperman J.W. Dorr visiting the area in 1860: "If St. Francisville is stronger on the ornamental, Bayou Sara is out of sight ahead of her on the

practical, for she does all the business and a great deal of business is done, too." http://files.usgwarchives.net/la/weeliciana/history/bsarah.txt, accessed March 15, 2015. See, also, "Louisiana in Slices. Parish of West Feliciana," *New Orleans Daily Crescent,* May 21, 1860; and Anne Butler and Norman C. Ferachi, *Images of America: St. Francisville and West Feliciana Parish* (Charleston, SC: Arcadia Publishing, 2014): 7–8.

79. Adelicia Acklen to Corinne Lawrence, November 28, 1857, MHP, TSLA.

80. *Springfield Republican,* November 29, 1858.

81. Henry M. Hayes to Oliver B. Hayes, Jr., November 1, 1858, McGavock-Hayes Family Papers Addition, 1796–2000, micro. 1677, TSLA.

82. Adelicia Acklen to Corinne Lawrence, December 28, 1858, MHP, TSLA.

83. Adelicia Acklen to Corinne Lawrence, November 28, 1857, MHP, TSLA.

84. Adelicia Acklen to Corinne Lawrence, February 13, 1859, MHP, TSLA

85. Adelicia Acklen to Corinne Lawrence, November 28, 1857, MHP, TSLA.

86. Adelicia Acklen to Corinne Lawrence, February 4, 1858, MHP, TLSA.

87. A Persac, *Norman's Chart of the Lower Mississippi River* (New Orleans: B.M. Norman, 1858.)

88. Adelicia Acklen to Corinne Lawrence, February 4, 1858, MHP, TSLA.

89. Adelicia Acklen to Corinne Lawrence, March 5, 1858, MHP, TSLA.

90. Adelicia Acklen to Corinne Lawrence, March 4, 1859, MHP, TSLA.

91. www.tngenweb.org/records/tn_wide/obits/nca/swca-10.htm; www.tngenweb.org/records/tn_wide/obits/nca/nca2-08.htm, accessed July 19, 2016.

92. Adelicia Acklen to Corinne Lawrence, February 13, 1859, MHP, TSLA.

93. Adelicia Acklen to Corinne Lawrence, April 8, 1860, MHP, TSLA.

94. Wardin, *Belmont Mansion,* 6.

95. Ibid, 9–10.

96. Kiser, "Scion of Belmont," Part I, 42.

97. Ibid, 41.

98. Ibid, 42.

99. John W. Kiser, "Scion of Belmont," Part II, *Tennessee Historical Quarterly* 38:1 (Spring 1979): 190.

100. Adelicia Acklen to Oliver B. Hayes, Jr., February 12, 1862, Hayes Family Papers, 1848–1888 (HFP), micro 1169–1,TSLA.

101. There are many good works on Nashville during the era of the U.S. Civil War. For general information see, for instance, Durham, *Reluctant Partners. Nashville and the Union, July 1, 1863 to June 30, 1865*; Stephen V. Ash, *Middle Tennessee Society Transformed, 1860–1870. War and Peace in the Upper South* (Knoxville: University of Tennessee Press, 2006); Wiley Sword, *The Confederacy's Last Hurrah. Spring Hill, Franklin, & Nashville* (Lawrence: University of Kansas Press, 1993); Stephen Ash, *When the Yankees Came* (Chapel Hill: University of North Carolina Press, 1995); and Stanley F. Horn, *The Decisive Battle of Nashville* (Baton Rouge: Louisiana State University Press, 1984.)

102. Laura F. Edwards, *Scarlett Doesn't Live Here Anymore. Southern Women in the Civil War Era* (Urbana: University of Illinois Press, 2000), 5.

103. LeeAnn Whites and Alecia P. Long, ed., *Occupied Women. Gender, Military Occupation, and the American Civil War* (Baton Rouge: Louisiana State University Press, 2009), 6.

104. Union ships began gathering near New Orleans in late 1861, Ash, *When the Yankees Came,* 14.

105. www.tngenweb.org/civilwar/csainf/cain34.html, accessed July 8, 2014.

106. Adelicia Acklen to Oliver B. Hayes, Jr., February 12, 1862, HFP, TSLA.

107. Ash, *Middle Tennessee Society Transformed,1860–1870,* 84–85; William L.B. Lawrence diary (Lawrence diary), February 23 and February 25, 1862, Lawrence Family Papers, 1780–1944 (LFP), Tennessee State Library and Archives (TSLA), Nashville.

108. Adelicia Acklen to Oliver B. Hayes, Jr., February 12, 1862, HFP, TSLA.

109. Adelicia Acklen to Oliver B. Hayes, Jr., undated, ca. July 1862, HFP, TSLA.

110. "Jim" is probably one of the slaves given to Acklen by her father at the time of her first marriage in 1839, also known as James Alexander, still with her in 1862. http://www.belmontmansion.com/#!index-of-enslaved-people/c22f6, accessed May 20, 2015.

111. Adelicia Acklen to Oliver B. Hayes, Jr., undated, ca. July 1862, HFP, TSLA.

112. Adelicia Acklen to Oliver B. Hayes, Jr., undated, ca. fall 1862, HFP, TSLA.

113. Peter Maslowski, *Treason Must Be Made Onerous. Military Occupation and Wartime Reconstruction in Nashville, Tennessee, 1862–65* (Millwood, N.Y.: KTO Press, 1978), 56–7.

114. Adelicia Acklen to Oliver B. Hayes, Jr., undated, ca. June 1863, HFP, TSLA.

115. Joseph A. S. Acklen to Adelicia Acklen, August 20, 1863, Acklen Papers, Special Collections, Howard Tilton Memorial Library, Tulane University, New Orleans, La.

116. See, Wardin, *Belmont Mansion*, 16–18; Mrs. John C. Gaut, "War Time Experiences at Franklin," Confederate Veteran 12:9 (September 1904): 422–3.

117. Annie Somers Gilchrist, *Some Representative Women of Tennessee* (Nashville: McQuiddy Printing Co., 1902): 165–168.

118. Catherine Clinton, *Tara Revisited: Women, War, & the Plantation Legend* (New York: Abbeville Press, 1995): 197

119. Gaut, "War Time Experiences at Franklin," 423.

120. Lt. & A.A.G. Jos. C. Robert to Adelicia Acklen, January 31, 1864, Davidson County Circuit Court, Loose Records, 1864, Metro Archives (MNA), Nashville.

121. Lt. Gen. Leonidas Polk, C.A.S., Order, March 23, 1864, Davidson County Circuit Court, Loose Records, 1864, MNA.

122. Brig. Gen. Thomas H. Taylor, C.A.S., Order, March 27, 1864, Davidson County Circuit Court, Loose Records, 1864, MNA.

123. Acting Lieutenant Cyrenius Dorning, U.S.N., Shipping Authorization, April 13, 1864, Davidson County Circuit Court, Loose Records, 1864, MNA; http://www.history.navy.mil/photos/images/h00001/h00513c.htm, accessed September 25, 2014.

124. Lt. & AAG Joseph C. Robert, C.S.A., to Col. Frank Powers, C.S.A., April 15, 1864, Camp Dick Garnett Letterbook, March 5–April 23, 1864, Special Collections, University of Mississippi Libraries, Oxford.

125. http://csatrainmen.com/PDF/CSA_StaffOfficers.pdf, accessed September 26, 2014.

126. United States. War Department, *The War of the Rebellion: A Compilation of the Official Records of the Union and Confederate Armies*, Series I, Vol. 52, Part II Supp. (Washington, D.C.: Government Printing Office, 1880–1901): 700.

127. K.R. Breese, Lieutenant Commander & Senior Naval Officer, U.S.N., "Shipping Notice," Davidson County Circuit Court, Loose Records, 1864, MNA.

128. *New York Times*, June 18, 1864.

129. Kiser, "Scion of Belmont," Part I, 44.

130. Durham, *Reluctant Partners*, 245–8; Horn, *The Decisive Battle of Nashville*.

131. Adelicia Acklen to Sarah Hayes, July 22, 1866, MHP, TSLA

132. Adelicia Acklen to Sarah Hayes, July 28, 1865, MHP, TSLA.

133. On departure from New York in the summer of 1865, Joseph was 16, William almost 10, Claude just turned 8, and Pauline not yet 6 years old.

134. *New York Herald,*, September 2,1865

135. Adelicia Acklen to Sarah Hayes, [1866], MHP, TSLA.

136. *Cincinnati Daily Gazette*, February 8, 1866. It is quite certain Sallie Acklen, and not six-year-old Pauline, accompanied Adelicia to this gala event.

137. Adelicia Acklen to Sarah Hayes, February 25, 1866, MHP, TSLA.

138. Ibid.

139. Adelicia Acklen to Corinne Lawrence, July 2, 1866, MHP, TSLA.

140. Adelicia Acklen to Sarah Hayes, July 22, 1866, MHP, TSLA.P,HH

141. Oliver B. Hayes, Jr., to Sallie Acklen Hoffman, September 27, 1866, HFP, TSLA.

142. Kiser, "Scion of Belmont," Part I, 44; Ancestry.com. New York, New York, Marriage Index 1866–1937 [database on-line], accessed August 8, 2016.

143. See, for instance, Frances Gibson Satterfield, *Madame LeVert: A Biography of Octavia Walton LeVert* (Atlanta: Edisto Publishing, 1987); and Octavia LeVert, *Souvenirs of Travel* (New York: S.H. Goetzel and Company, 1857.)

144. "Southern Hospitality," *Republican Banner*, December 19, 1866.

145. *Springfield Republican*, July 1867. In this article, the newspaper misidentified Dr. Cheatham as "ex-Rebel Gen. Cheatham."

146. Wardin, *Belmont Mansion*, 23.

147. Marriage Contract of Adelicia Acklen and W.A. Cheatham, Marriage Book 5, page 465, Nashville Public Library, Nashville.

148. See, for instance, Thomas J. Brown, *Dorothea Dix: New England Reformer* (Cambridge: Harvard University Press, 1998.)

149. See, for instance, *The Syracuse New York Daily Standard,* May 13, 1863; Octavia Zollicoffer Bond, "Yester Nashville Names: The Cheatham Family," *The Nashville American,* August 22, 1909; Kay Baker Gaston, "A World Overturned: The Civil War Experience of Dr. William A. Cheatham and His Family," *Tennessee Historical Quarterly* 50 (Spring 1991): 3–16; "William A. Cheatham," *The Tennessee Encyclopedia of History and Culture,* ver. 2.0, http://tennesseeencyclopedia.net/entry.php?rec=236, accessed August 9, 2016.

150. Adelicia Cheatham to Mattie Cheatham, November 22, 1868, Private collection of Mary Williamson Parrent.

151. "A Big Present," *Nashville Union and Dispatch,* July 7, 1867.

152. "New Year's Call," *Daily American,* January 1, 1876.

153. *Feliciana Sentinel*, December 1, 1877.

154. Lease between Robertson Yeatman, agent and attorney-in-fact for Adelicia Acklen and John O. Friend and Burrell Lanier, Notarial Record "O", 1865–1867, West Feliciana Clerk of Court Records, West Feliciana Parish, St. Francisville, La.

155. "Cotton Plantations for Rent," *Nashville Union & Dispatch,* March 3, 1867.

156. Kiser, "Scion of Belmont, Part II, 195.

157. Adelicia Cheatham to Corinne Lawrence, December 27, 1871, MHP, TSLA.

158. Adelicia Cheatham to Corinne Lawrence, February 3, 1872, HFP, TSLA.

159. Wardin, *Belmont Mansion,* 30.

160. Kiser, "Scion of Belmont, Part II, 194–5.

161. Adelicia Cheatham to Corinne Lawrence, February 3, 1872, HFP, TSLA.

162. Purchase Agreement between Adelicia Cheatham and William H. Acklen and Samuel L. James and Louis Trager, Notarial Records "S", 1878–1882, West Feliciana Clerk of Court Records, West Feliciana Parish, St. Francisville, La. William Acklen sold his interest in the Louisiana properties with this agreement as well.

163. *Evening Star* (Washington, D.C.), December 26, 1885.

164. *Evening Star,* April 28, 1887.

165. "Death of Mrs. Cheatham," *Critic Record* (Washington, D.C.), May 5, 1887; *Daily Advocate* (Baton Rouge), May 6, 1887.

166. Wardin, *Belmont Mansion,* 32. W.A. Cheatham, still Adelicia's husband at the time of her death, lived until 1900. Cheatham is also buried at Mount Olivet, not in the Acklen vault, and next to his first wife, Mary Ready Cheatham. http://findagrave.com/cgi-bin/fg.cgi?page=pv&GRid=21013707&PIpi=21221426, accessed August 5, 2016.

167. Kiser, "Scion of Belmont, Part II, 200.

Belmont Mansion: An Icon of the American Country House Movement

By Jerry Trescott

Stand today upon the edge of the limestone terrace in front of Belmont Mansion, enjoying the shade of mature trees on a summer's day, raise your head up and down, then move it side to side and back and forth. All the while be sure your eyes are wide open and your astute powers of observation are working overtime. You will need all of your faculties to take in what lies before you. Rest assured you are only one of thousands since 1853 who have stood in that exact spot, dazzled by the splendor before them. Along with antebellum international visitors, to Union soldiers on guard during the Civil War, to school girls dreaming of the future, to modern tourists, then yourself, you have now joined a long line of admirers of Belmont Mansion.

Understanding a structure this complex requires multiple disciplines. It is not enough to simply walk through room after room viewing assembled furnishings in restored settings. An architectural analysis of Belmont Mansion cannot be attempted without attaining insight into who its builders, the Acklens, were and what they represented for their time and place in American history.

Joseph and Adelicia Hayes Franklin Acklen played equal roles in the development of Belmont, one the dreamer, while the other possessed organizational abilities to make their combined vision a reality. It goes without saying who initially funded the purchase of land upon which their estate was to rise. The young widow Adelicia Franklin was left without a husband at the age of twenty-nine in 1846. Franklin applied an immense inherited fortune to amassing property on which she developed a most amazing ante-bellum country estate. Franklin's primary influence feeding her desire to establish a country estate was the home she left behind in Sumner County.

Fairvue, the home Franklin shared with her late husband Isaac Franklin, was for its time an immense neo-Palladian structure with a broad central hall from which opened numerous parlors on the

Thousands of people have been dazzled by the splendor of Belmont since 1853, Adelicia Acklen's summer estate on a hill south of downtown Nashville. (Belmont Mansion Association)

first floor, with spacious chambers above. The Franklins saw the need immediately after marriage to enlarge Fairvue yet again, into what then would have been one of the largest houses in Sumner County. Fairvue's square footage nearly doubled, incorporating a new kitchen with accompanying service areas.

With Isaac Franklin's death in 1846, it would not have been unusual for Adelicia to retreat entirely from the realities of widowhood into a more private world. In the short period of four and one half weeks Franklin lost not only her husband, but two of her three surviving children to childhood diseases. Just a year after Isaac's death, Adelicia left behind her grief-filled plantation in Summer County for the presumed safety and companionship of her parents in Nashville.

Shortly after arriving in Nashville, Franklin purchased a brick Greek Revival townhouse on Cherry Street (now Fourth Avenue North). Similar in plan and form to the house in which she had been born in 1817, Franklin would own this property for the remainder of her life. Even after moving to Belmont, Franklin is known to have maintained the Nashville house as an investment property.

For the majority of her young life, Adelicia Hayes Franklin enjoyed the pleasantries of estate living. Oliver B. Hayes, Adelicia's father, purchased his own estate, known as Rokeby, south of Nashville in 1827 (demolished 1949), while Adelicia was still a child. Outside her windows at Rokeby sweeping lawns led to flower gardens featuring a vine covered gateway.[1] Isaac Franklin's two thousand acre Fairvue estate boasted extensive landscaped grounds and greenhouses for Adelicia Franklin's enjoyment. Sights, sounds and smells of one of the fastest growing cities in the south, were a far different atmosphere for the young widow.

When Franklin inherited a fortune over which she had complete control, plans were quickly formulated for the creation of yet another estate. Think of Rokeby and Fairvue as her primary inspiration, certainly not architecturally, for the new Belmont was in an entirely different style, but unquestionably one for the lifestyle a country estate afforded. In retrospect the progression in Franklin's life from one estate to another, leading to Belmont's development as the antebellum south's premiere country estate, can easily be documented.

Nashville in the 1840s expanded hastily in multiple directions. This seems to have been especially true to the south, as residential development led to the creation of new political wards.[2] Some of the most attractive land lay to the south as evidenced by the creation of the Oliver B. Hayes estate, Rokeby. Just to the south of Rokeby on adjacent land, Adelicia Franklin's uncle, Leven Browning, constructed a small neo-classical country house. This structure was unique in form to Tennessee, as surviving evidence has shown. Within a decade Browning's brick house succumbed to fire, leaving a hilltop scarred with what we presume to have been a smoke stained empty shell.

How convenient for the widow Franklin, a rich young woman with the wherewithal to build where, when, and how she chose, that a building site was available on one of the highest hills in Nashville. Since ancient times, for both defense and visibility, people of means have sought hilltops on which to construct forts, castles, then country houses when civilization progressed to a more peaceful society. Most importantly, in Nashville summers, breezes flowed up and over hills and valleys, then into and out of houses with proper alignment to those breezes.

Hilltop sites were highly sought by Nashvillians able to afford houses similar to Leven Browning's. Franklin left behind no diaries or journals relaying her thoughts as she accumulated land for her Belmont estate. What is known, in the spring of 1849, the soon to be Mrs. Joseph Alexander Smith Acklen purchased the site of her uncle's burned out house. Other contiguous tracts of land were combined in an attempt to expand the boundaries of her hilltop estate, eventually reaching 177 acres.

One of the primary occupants of the new Belmont would be Adelicia's second husband Joseph, a native of Huntsville, Alabama, where he had recently served as the federal prosecutor for northern Alabama. Only one year older than his bride, Joseph was Adelicia's contemporary, while Isaac Franklin had been twenty-eight years Adelicia's senior.

Once the Acklens secured land for Belmont, the question of what type of house to build naturally came into question. Masonry walls presented a solidity and permanence far outweighing any wooden structure. The factor of surviving walls from the Browning residence played into this decision. Should the site be cleared entirely, or would building within the shell of the previous dwelling possibly be an option? The Acklens and modern researchers have both been perplexed by this question when delving into the architectural evolution of Belmont Mansion. Early recorders of Belmont assumed, erroneously it has turned out, that the Acklens were the first to build upon the hill, or if not the first that the site was cleared prior to commencement of construction.

To adequately interpret the design and metamorphosis of Belmont, one must first comprehend the Acklens' choice to build within the shell of the house built by her uncle. Today we would likely hastily clear the ruins, moving on, not with repair, but new construction. Exhaustive research has failed to reveal the date of the fire that destroyed Browning's villa.

Having made the decision to repair, rebuild, and enlarge, the primary concern for the Acklens would have been the stability of the Browning house's remaining walls. This factor depended upon the length of time those walls were exposed to weather. Contingent on how long the building stood open, freeze/thaw patterns could have had disastrous implications for blending old walls into new construction.

Brick making in this period had advanced little from ancient times. Clay, the natural product utilized in the process, was still packed into wooden brick molds, sun-dried, then fired in a kiln. Primitive kilns constructed, primarily of the bricks themselves, were fueled by a wood fire laid in the center for firing or curing the brick. As stacked, bricks closest to the fire were exposed to the greatest amount of heat, assuring the hardest brick for use in an exterior wall. In exterior loadbearing brick construction, "hard fired" bricks were laid in different structural bonds, such as Common, English, or Flemish. "Soft fired" bricks furthest from the fire, were meant for interior load bearing walls. Exposed to weather "soft fired" bricks quickly deteriorate, turning to powder.

Various phases of restoration at Belmont Mansion have led to major plaster repairs in several rooms. Exposed evidence proves conclusively that smoke

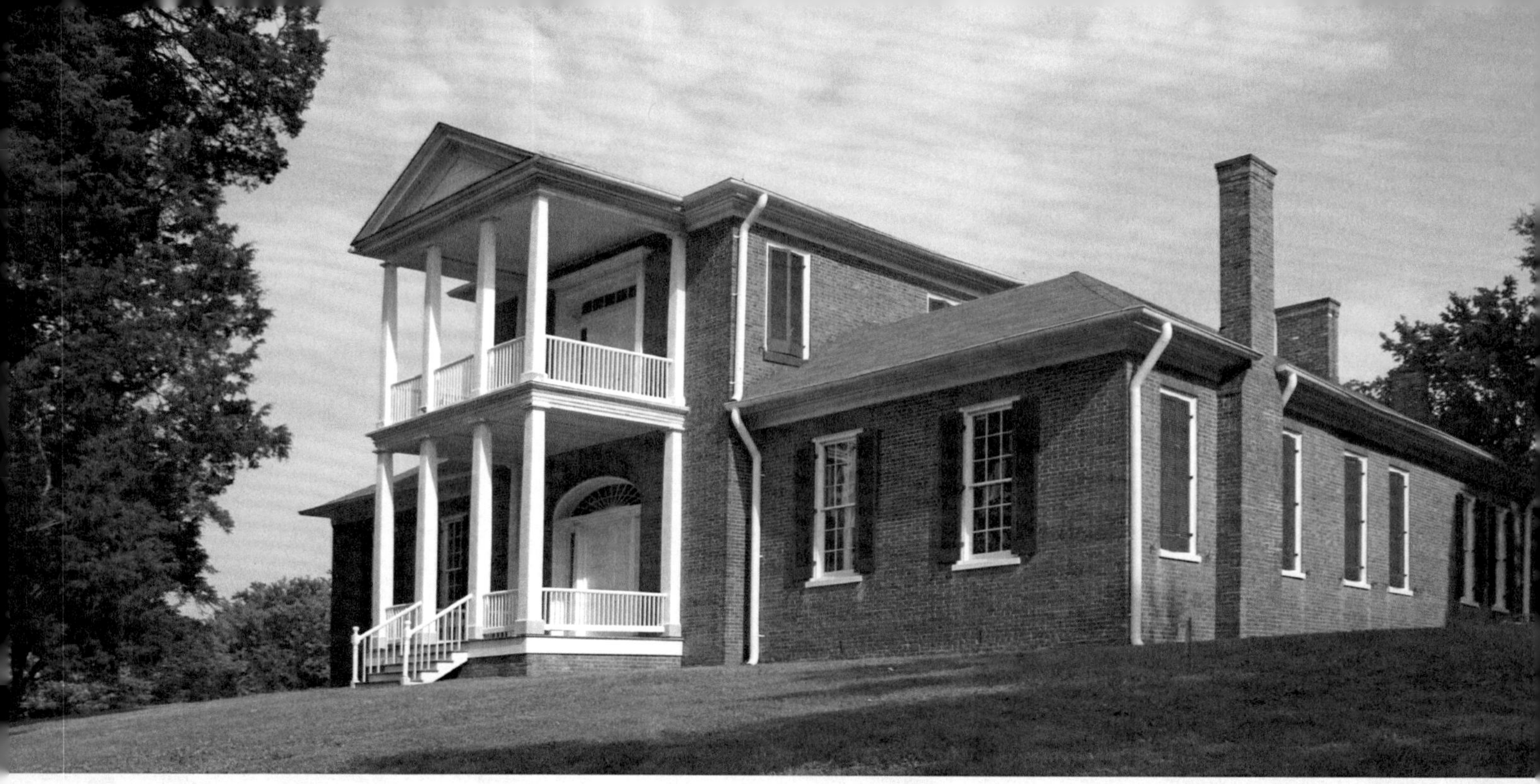

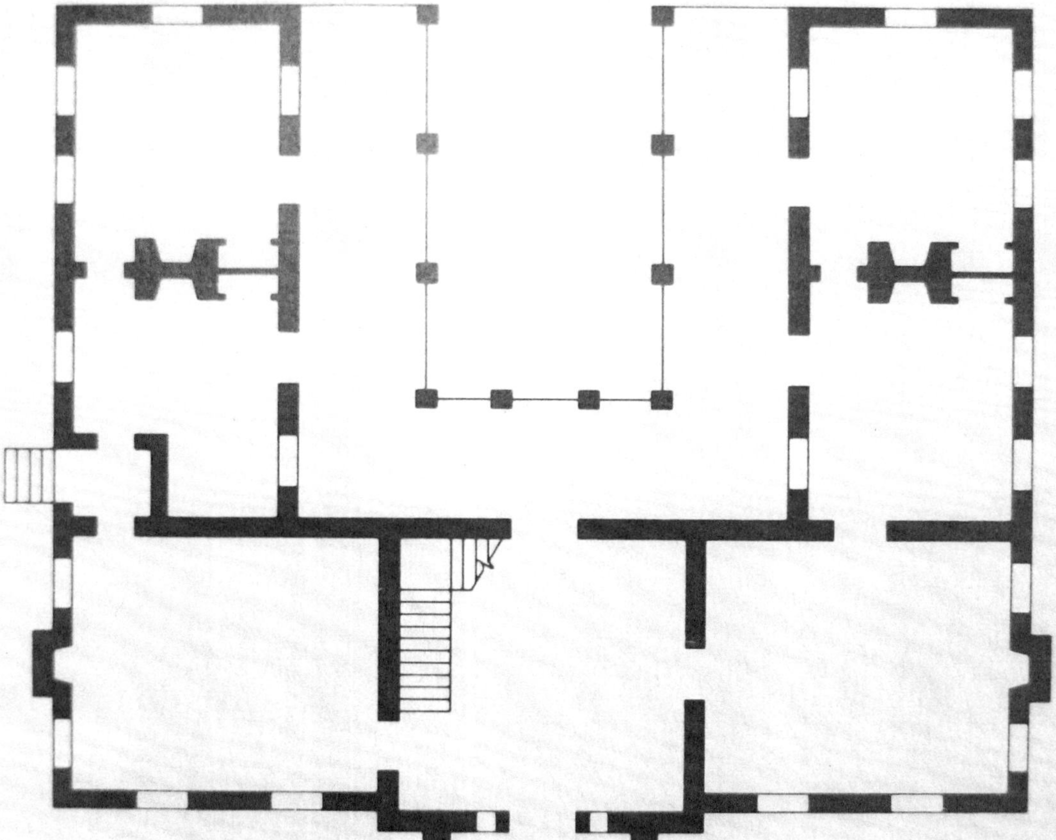

stained walls of the Browning era were incorporated into Belmont during the Acklen construction period.

Surviving architectural evidence suggests Leven Browning built a neo-Palladian villa. Examples of the style are the early form of Monticello, the Semple house in Williamsburg Virginia, the Sally Billy house and the Williams-Reid-Macon house in Halifax, North Carolina, all of which exhibit a form representative of Browning's home. The similarities between the first Belmont and these examples are primarily a two story central pavilion, flanked by one story wings raised upon a high pedestal or foundation.

Most striking in similarity to the Acklens' home is a house in rural Alabama, outside of Tuscumbia, surprisingly also known as Belle Mont. Constructed for a transplanted Virginian, Alexander Mitchell, from 1828–1832, this restored example of neo-Palladian style offers a plan similar to the u-shaped plan of the 1853 Belmont.[3] This style, first popular in America prior to the Revolution, arrived with settlers from over the mountains coming to the "old southwest" of Tennessee and Alabama. Palladian houses, an easy form to build in brick or frame, were designed to capture breezes in either its original region, the Veneto of Italy, or high upon a Tennessee hill.

One indication of a simpler plan for Browning's villa came to light during plaster restoration on the second floor of the existing mansion in the 1990s. With the removal of failing plaster in what is now Adelicia Acklen's bedroom, a line of joist pockets were revealed at waist height. This discovery documents the Browning house supported wings (today's central parlor and library), exhibiting a shed roof rather than the typical gable end as found in such houses. The angle of these roofs ran from the one story eave line upward, until making contact with the side walls of the two story central section.

Further plaster repairs in the library and central parlor, where yet more failing plaster was removed, indicate a brutal fire. Smoke stains survive on what would have been the east and west one-story walls of the wings. A westerly wind blew the fire across and through the house, burning out windows on the western elevation. Exterior smoke stains remain to this day beneath Acklen-period stucco. Fire lapped through window embrasures in masonry walls, documenting the west wall was much more involved than the east.

Browning's smaller, more compact, classical villa became history, literally lost

Belmont incorporates an earlier brick house that burned in the 1840s. Architectural evidence suggests it was a neo-Palladian villa, similar to the 1828-1833 Belle Mont near Tuscumbia, Alabama, which was built in a u-shaped plan. (Belle Mont, HABS, Library of Congress, and floorplan, from *Architecture of the Old South: Mississippi and Alabama*.)

to the flames of time. Suffice it to say certain portions of the Browning house survived as detailed by existing evidence in restored areas, as well as the basement below. It was within that space, previously home to Leven Browning and his wife Lucinda Hightower, that Belmont was planned and built by the Acklens.

By the spring of 1850, Joseph and Adelicia Acklen were preparing to celebrate their first anniversary, the birth of their first child, Joseph Hayes Acklen, (born May 20, 1850) plus planning their new home. The 1850 United States Census lists a number of workers already living on the property, including ten African-Americans.[4] We can be sure that by the summer of 1850 materials were assembled and construction was underway.

Multiple nationalities and races are well represented by talented workers in any era. Skilled workers were just as likely to be African American as recent immigrants. The antebellum south made use of enslaved peoples in broader tasks than field workers or house servants. It is unrealistic to believe Belmont could or would have been constructed without the labor of enslaved workmen. Certainly clearing of the site would have been accomplished by Acklen slaves, listed as having been on site in 1850. The first weeks required intense labor as damaged walls came down and new foundations were dug for the expansion. As work proceeded, more highly skilled labor was required. Those skills were often found within a local labor force including enslaved people. Owners of enslaved laborers were known to lease out services of a black carpenter or mason to master builders, just as they would any other piece of property. Builders choosing enslaved workers had the option of ownership or leasing. Leasing workers was often viewed as a more efficient way of doing business.

George Steele, a builder in Huntsville, Alabama, Joseph Acklen's birthplace, owned eleven slaves; two carpenters, five bricklayers, one stonecutter, and three plasterers.[5] Steele is an excellent example of a professional builder with a successful practice who utilized the labors of his own personal workforce. Steele's example was matched by builders and cabinetmakers throughout the south. *DeBow's Commercial Review*, a chronicle of all things southern in the antebellum period listed, four architects, 247 carpenters, twenty-seven brickmasons, seventeen stonemasons, eight stonecutters, seven lime-makers, thirty-two brickmakers, sixteen house plasterers, plus twenty-three painters and paperhangers all operating in Nashville in 1846.[6]

The axis of the ruined Browning house appears to have been south to north taking advantage of prevailing breezes. Belmont from the first was designed to take advantage of this gift from nature.

Predominating winds, originating in the southwest, speedily climbed Belmont's hill, ultimately pushing through, up, and around any residence built upon the hilltop.

Adelicia Acklen's Nashville townhouse was certainly closely surrounded by similar houses and commercial establishments. Moving to town from the pastoral atmosphere of Fairvue, to the frenetic activity of downtown Nashville city could not have been a pleasant transition. Fairvue most certainly offered far healthier and pleasurable conditions for Acklen's family.

Popular belief in the nineteenth century perpetuated the conviction that many fatal diseases were air-born. Putrid inner city air was believed to be the cause of multiple deaths in times of cholera and yellow fever epidemics. City dwellers of means choose to remove themselves to the country during dangerous months when such diseases were rampant. Former president James K. Polk, just weeks after attending the Acklen wedding in May of 1849, fell victim to cholera. A few years before Adelicia Franklin Acklen had lost two children to disease.

It is no wonder Acklen, now remarried, carrying yet another child, chose to spend a portion of her new wealth building a country house in an attempt to escape pestilence in the city two miles away. This was a fair distance in the 1850s. Such a trip would take an average person approximately an hour on foot, and less than thirty minutes when traveling by carriage. Residing at Belmont the Acklens would be a safe distance from infectious diseases, yet close enough to participate in business and social activities on their newly acquired hilltop.

From ancient times to the end of the country house era in the early twentieth century, spectacular views became paramount when planning a new dwelling. The selection of an elevated site provided relaxing views of unchanged landscape near and far. Surviving photos taken from Belmont's roof in the 1890s reveal an unspoiled landscape of tree-covered hills to the south. To the north the Acklens overlooked a rapidly expanding Nashville still surrounded by a swath of green. Strickland's Tennessee State Capitol, one of the most important structures in the new nation, could be seen rising in the distance.

What better prospect could this young couple expect to find than the land in which Adelicia Acklen was investing? Their view extended for miles in any direction, meaning Belmont would also be visible for that same distance. The site was perfect for innumerable reasons, least of which was the northern boundary of their assembled property touched the southern edge of Rokeby, Acklen's father's estate. To the east lay Hillside, the property of sister Corinne Hayes and her husband William Lawrence. Here in the southeast quadrant of Nashville an expansive family complex was taking root with houses rising upon the horizon. None however were quite like Belmont, of this the Acklens were sure, and soon, so would everyone else in Nashville.

Human nature has changed little since ancient times. Patricians in Rome, the rising merchant class in Renaissance Europe, as well as newly enriched Nashvillians in the antebellum period, all had the capacity to show jealousy. Each citizen of 1850s Nashville speedily became aware of a new house rising before their eyes two miles in the distance. With a population of just under 17,000 people, neighbors and strangers alike were keenly aware of the Acklens progress as the house grew taller, brick by brick, upon the Acklens' hill.[7] People who had no conception of building costs naturally assumed the new Mrs. Acklen was well on her way to spending Isaac Franklin's entire fortune for the creation of Belmont. Locals began to refer to the house, then the entire estate as, "The Acklen Folly," no doubt blaming the new husband for the expense, for he was most definitely not a native Tennessean.[8]

Gossip aside, the Acklens pushed forward through three successive building seasons from 1850 to 1853, first occupying Belmont by the summer of 1853. This is verified by the date of a letter addressed to Joseph Acklen at Belmont from a business associate in an attempt to reach him at that location or any other.[9]

No house springs from the earth totally free from influences that have gone before. Multiple architectural fashions were swirling around the Acklens in the spring of 1850. Just south of Strickland's capitol sat one of the most prominent and discussed building projects in Nashville's history, Polk Place, home of former president James K. Polk and his wife Sarah Childress.

Before leaving Washington the Polks purchased a large city lot containing a house built by the late Felix Grundy, which by the 1840s had become terribly out of fashion for so conspicuous a location. The Polks instigated a building campaign enlarging the house, making it over in the Greek Revival style, with the addition of a monumental portico on one elevation, and a porch *an' antis* on the south side. It is this elevation that ties Polk Place to the Belmont additions of 1850–53.

There is more than a fleeting similarity between the southern elevation of Polk Place as completed in 1849 with the southern façade of Belmont as completed in 1853. Both feature a recessed porch with monumental fluted columns exhibiting Corinthian capitals. To the rear of the columns stretching across the width of both recessed porches are balconies. Cast iron railing, practically identical to that on Belmont's balcony is evident in an historic photograph of Polk Place.[10] Identical full height pilasters rise to the height of this porch giving visual strength to this element. Framing the exterior corners

This façade of Polk Place, completed in 1849, may have inspired the very similar façade at Belmont, completed in 1853. The cast iron railing at the two mansions is almost identical. (Wiles photo, from *History of Homes and Gardens of Tennessee*, 1936)

of both buildings are two more identical pilasters. Resting upon capitals of both columns and pilasters, a broad cornice consisting of a deep fascia and projecting soffit complete the design of Polk Place.

An almost identical arrangement of elements can be found at Belmont. Notable exceptions are the addition of classical trims, dentils, and modillions on Belmont's façade, all an indication of the Acklens' wealth. Such happenstance rarely occurs in architecture. One structure usually influences the design of another. The Polks were closely associated with the Acklens. Joseph and Adelicia Acklen would have had more than a passing interest in the transformation of the Polks' home. Adelicia Acklen and Sarah Polk remained friends until Acklen's death in 1887.

No better architectural inspiration existed in all of Nashville during this era than the new home of a former president. The homes and lifestyles of American presidents have been closely followed since Washington first took the oath of office in 1789. Certainly every master carpenter in the state was capable of producing these elements, and did so on many houses. Simply put, there are too many similarities existing between both houses for there not to be a connection. A surviving photo of Polk Place validates this theory.

James Patrick in his notable work, *Architecture in Tennessee,* published in 1981, cites a native Tennessean, James M. Hughes born in 1818, as the master builder of Polk Place.[11] Hughes, according to Patrick, enjoyed a successful career into the late 1850s and beyond into the post-war period.

In tracking Hughes's career, Patrick speaks of projects prior to Polk Place, for which he drew a floor plan in 1848, and after 1853, leaving a substantial gap.[12] Polk Place was substantially complete by 1849. As work at Polk Place came to a halt, the next major residential construction project in Nashville became Belmont in 1850. It would have been natural for a talented master builder to migrate from one site to another, particularly with the connection between the two families. The career of James M. Hughes may well have included Belmont in the three-year period from 1850 to 1853. Both houses were large dwellings requiring a large talented labor force. Hughes would have had such a force at his fingertips having just completed Polk Place. His skilled crew could have easily made the transition from one site to another, especially since the buildings were similar in form.

The Acklens were also influenced in their choice of an architectural style by Romantic designs just making their way to Nashville. Most influential in this period were the forms of Italy, giving rise to the Italian Villa style with which Belmont is identified. The completed Belmont of 1860 most resembles this emerging architectural idiom and it transition from Palladian Villa to Italian Villa was a multi-step process beginning in 1850. In the ensuing ten years, multiple minds and hands contributed to this evolution.

Master builders, aided by many American treatises of architectural styles and plans, were capable of designing and fulfilling the needs of all clients. Nashville profited substantially from the talents of these semi-professionals in an age before America began professionally training architects. This was a time when gentlemen participated enthusiastically in the design process of their domestic quarters. Educated men prided themselves on an ability to speak and act intelligently on questions of architecture.

Joseph Acklen was just that, an educated client, determined to build his vision upon Adelicia Acklen's hilltop.

Acklen profited from both an academy and university education in the second quarter of the nineteenth century when the classics were a featured course of study.[13] No letters or plans survive from this first phase of construction to document his involvement. Our only understanding of Joseph Acklen's influence and participation in the project was written four years after his death. Elizabeth Fries Ellet, author of *Queens of American Society* published in 1867, when writing about Adelicia Acklen, relates that Joseph, "possessing refined taste and cultivation, made improvements in their large estate near Nashville, building a magnificent house…"[14]

Young men, such as Joseph Acklen, often studied the Greek language.[15] Ancient democracy was heavily promoted, the age of Pericles being touted as an ideal. The revolution in Greece during the 1820s brought these thoughts to the forefront, inspiring young men and women alike. Such events, coupled with a metamorphosis in architectural styles brought about the construction of Greek "Temples" in various domestic forms worldwide. New York author James Fenimore Cooper is known to have written in 1838, "The public sentiment just now runs almost exclusively and popularly into the Grecian school. We build little besides temples for our churches and banks, our taverns, our courthouses, and our dwellings."[16]

By 1850, the popularity of those staid Greek Revival temple forms, now a generation old, with classical details pasted upon them, was beginning to wane. The introduction of more romantic styles began to dot the nation's horizon, aided by the publications of Andrew Jackson Downing, who offered both architectural and landscape designs.

In Nashville, a city far from the east coast, fashionable architectural styles were at times slower to develop. Architects traveling from the east, even from across the Atlantic, became the first to design and develop more fashionable up to date structures.[17] Few American neoclassical houses were designed without the direct influence of European trained architects such as Benjamin Latrobe, who did not stop in Nashville, (although he is known to have supplied drawings for a dwelling there) on his way to New Orleans before dying there of yellow fever in 1820.[18] This constant movement of talented well-trained men benefited Nashville. Many lingered long enough to leave a lasting impression upon the built environment, using the city as a waystation before heading further south.

William Strickland was called to Nashville in 1845 for the construction of the State Capitol on a hill then known as Cedar Knob, thereby creating a permanent example of his genius.[19] What he did not accomplish was the design and building of Belmont Mansion as stated by historians of earlier eras. Not a shred of stylistic or written evidence exists to lend credence to this outdated theory. The

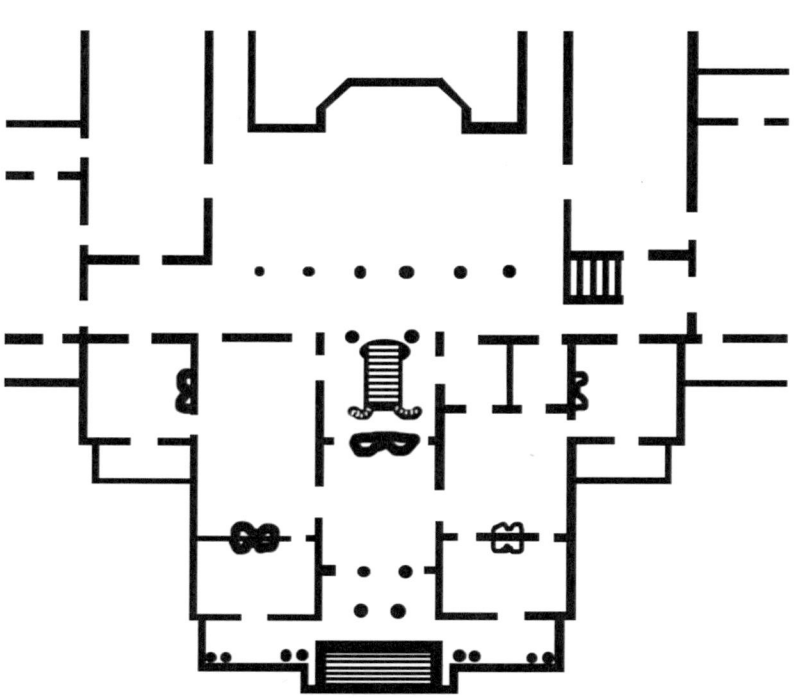

Belmont's square front hall was a design change from the earlier Browning house. The space provided perfect architectural balance, (Photo by Edward Houck and floor plan detail, Belmont Mansion Association)

completed 1853, phase one Belmont, was likely a large rather boxy house straddling the crest of the hill with a minimum of architectural ornament. As seen today, the last two extensions to the sides, both east and west, completing the principal façade, had not yet been built.

Plantation income allowed for the niceties of Joseph and Adelicia Acklen's existence. In the short period from Isaac Franklin's death in 1846 to the spring of 1851, plantation income amounted to $507,137.97 with which to finance Belmont's construction.[20] The house was repaired, enlarged, and rebuilt during 1850–1853. As a late Federal neo-Palladian villa the Browning house contained fewer rooms than required by the Acklens. When analyzing Belmont, keep in mind how architecture was adapted for the southern climate. What had previously been a tight small brick house with small window openings, the new Belmont was amazingly different, becoming a light and air-filled creation. Influenced by an Italian Renaissance interpretation of an ancient plan, filtered by way of the English Renaissance a hundred years later, to the final, less formal American arrangement of rooms and details generations later, grew the nucleus of the Belmont we know today.[21]

Entire walls were rebuilt rather than just punching through to enlarge window and door openings. Of note the south facing wall containing the principle entry was entirely rebuilt beginning in 1850. As found today three 10' 3" tall openings stand side by side, accounting for approximately 80% of wall surface. With two operable transoms, two sets of French doors, plus the entry door, little solid wall surface remains. A majority of the wall opens to allow cooling breezes to enter the house. The addition of French doors and operable transoms indicates extensive restructuring occurred during the 1850–1853 building period giving new dimension to the structure.

Just as President Andrew Jackson raised his ceilings after the 1834 Hermitage fire in order to create a more formal, grander house than had previously existed, it is likely the Acklens chose to do the same. By the 1850s, Nashville had become a much larger, more sophisticated society than existed during the age of Jackson. Modern expectations for houses made the luxuries of the 1830s seem a necessity. Population had doubled from 1830 to 1850, bringing with it an East Coast awareness of new technology and culture unseen in the social order of the expanding frontier of years past.[22] Higher ceilings meant cooler rooms, which was the aim of building on such a site in the first place.

Inspired by Palladian forms, Belmont's square entry is central to any discussion of the Browning house or the Acklen reconstruction. A perfect architectural balance exists in the placement of double leaf doors on the east and west walls leading into today's central parlor and library.

French doors in the south exterior wall were originally balanced by another pair in the north wall, also opening to the exterior, prior to the construction of the salon in 1859. Directly opposite the entry door stands a projecting chimney breast on the north wall. Each perfectly spaced element complements another on an opposite wall, whether that be east, west, north, or south, a symbol of classical rigidity as yet unbroken by the asymmetry of more romantic styles just coming into vogue.

The Acklens never intended to occupy their Belle Monte, as they referred to the estate early on, as a year-round residence. Winters were spent on the plantation in Louisiana, with numerous sojourns to New Orleans. Viewed primarily as a summer home, stairs would have been of secondary importance to other more impressive architectural elements, including marble mantels and elaborate classical ceiling medallions depicting bulging acanthus leaves.

The placement of stairs on an exterior gallery would seem typical to people who frequented New Orleans several times a year. Gallery stairs were long a common feature of French Creole architecture, especially on close knit city lots. Belmont's early stairs would likely have risen from the rear gallery, but still under protection of the roof. Centered on a broad rear gallery, a large niche was created in the 1850–1853 construction period. The early Belmont stair likely stood within this space as does its grander 1859 replacement. Above stairs, a shorter open gallery provided excellent views of Nashville while functioning as a connector to multiple family bedrooms.

Belmont as configured in 1853 in actuality had a much more of a deep south flavor than the completed house of 1859–1860. The aforementioned gallery adjacent to the principal floor was long and broad, running the length of the northern elevation. In this early form the gallery was open-ended both to the east and west. Later additions completely enclosed this space. Positioned as it was, the gallery took full advantage of any available breeze originating from multiple directions.

Galleries such as the one created by the Acklens were frequently treated as outdoor living spaces, furnished much the same as modern Americans would treat a screened porch in 2017. From this gallery major first floor rooms were easily accessed. Doors leading to the rear gallery were generally aligned with similar openings on the principle façade, allowing for the passage of air through each living space. On certain days a table may well have been brought to the gallery for dining. This comfortable, always shaded, open aired gallery would have been one of most relaxing, friendly and heavily utilized spaces in the early years of Belle Monte.

For centuries country house life represented a unique lifestyle for limited quantities of people. The building of a country house was not merely an instance of a family seeking shelter. Such endeavors served as an announcement to contemporaries that the occupant had arrived, both financially and socially. Belmont, as it rose from newly laid foundations became a statement easily read by all. The Acklens designed, lived in, entertained in, and enjoyed one of the most uniquely planned houses yet built in Nashville. Those fortunate enough to cross the threshold also participated in the enjoyment of their lifestyle.

A completely different house, with little indication of what had come before rose upon the hilltop. This more modern residence was emblematic of the times is which the Acklens lived. Breaking out of an earlier more classical shell brought an outmoded derelict house to useful life once again. At some point in the process it was decided that merely raising the wings to a full second story would not provide enough chamber space above stairs. Small, low ceilinged rooms were far from what the Acklens sought from the project. What had formerly been a colloquial form of Palladio, the much simpler Browning house evolved into a more studied Renaissance plan with the Acklen additions.

On either side of the original, centrally located projecting pavilion, in front of what were originally shed-roofed wings, two full height, two-story additions were joined to the existing structure.[23] Within each addition were two new rooms, one up and one down, for a total of four rooms. The Italians referred to such private spaces as "Cabinet Rooms," a term Americans seldom made use of either on house plans or in conversation. The inclusion of such spaces in Belmont's revised floor plan, created unique, individual specialized rooms, then becoming fashionable in America. These smaller more intimate spaces often featured the display of artwork and personal collections.

Palladio developed his cabinet rooms in a very specific way. In his second of four books of architecture, twelve designs are featured offering the type of plan developed by the Acklens.[24] Many of Palladio's Italian villas featured recessed double height porches allowing for the inclusion of cabinet rooms into the design. Falling to the right and left of the principle entry, each room offered access to the exterior, hence Belmont's three doors opening onto the recessed entry porch. Interior plans as designed by Palladio offered long broad rooms often attached to the rear of such spaces. In America these rooms were utilized as parlors, or libraries, identical to spaces located within the completed Belmont. These cabinet room additions, placed to the right and left of the former projecting pavilion squared up the main block of the house totally eliminating the earlier lines of Browning's villa. This "squaring up" of the new Belmont allowed for the construction of a continuous classical cornice wrapping the structure, adding to the striking resemblance early Belmont shared with Polk Place.

Belmont's Palladio inspired additions brought the mass of the structure forward beyond the original building line. The two story recess created by these additions became the porch an' antis seen today. Two monumental fluted columns topped by Corinthian capitals are centered within that recess. Pilasters flank both the interior and exterior corners of the additions bringing the entire façade into an architectural harmony of classical details. A balcony runs at the second story level from one wall to another just to the rear of the columns. The balconies' cast iron railing features classical motifs of repeating lyres and acanthus leaves.

From a distance this new assemblage of brick masses would not have presented an imposing profile from any direction. Alleviating this problem during the same building campaign (1850–1853), it appears the first Acklen wings made an appearance, expanding the house to both east and west, visually reducing the vertical bulk of the main block, while balancing the whole.

Structural evidence suggests these one story wings were added to the main block during the same construction period as the two story cabinet room additions. Both the "Tête-á-Tête" room and the winter parlor feature a flat inset panel below the double-hung sash windows. These window panels exhibit identical trims indicating a shared construction date. When complete the west wing likely became what is today interpreted as the winter parlor, while the east wing we believe was utilized as a dining room.

Across the rear gallery, in line with the newly added wings, stood two small outbuildings believed to date from the Browning era. Architectural evidence suggests one structure to the east, directly across from the probable 1850 dining room, functioned as a kitchen building before and during the Acklen era. On the lower level an enclosed deep, wide chimney breast is located. In the pre-Acklen era cooking would have been done on an open fire at this location, while the Acklens likely purchased a newly designed cast iron kitchen range.

Social obligations often lie at the root of multiple building projects and additions. This is where the Acklens found themselves as their wealth and standing expanded exponentially during the 1850s. The 1850 dining room was double the size of many conventional dining rooms in pre-war Nashville, but in time it proved too small for the Acklens. The city as Belmont's construction began was filled with narrow, deep, brick houses dating from the 1820s to the 1840s, as viewed in historic photos of the city.[25] Entertainments of large groups simply were not possible in such restricted quarters.

A ready and logical solution for Belmont became the enlargement of the kitchen building, with the addition of a

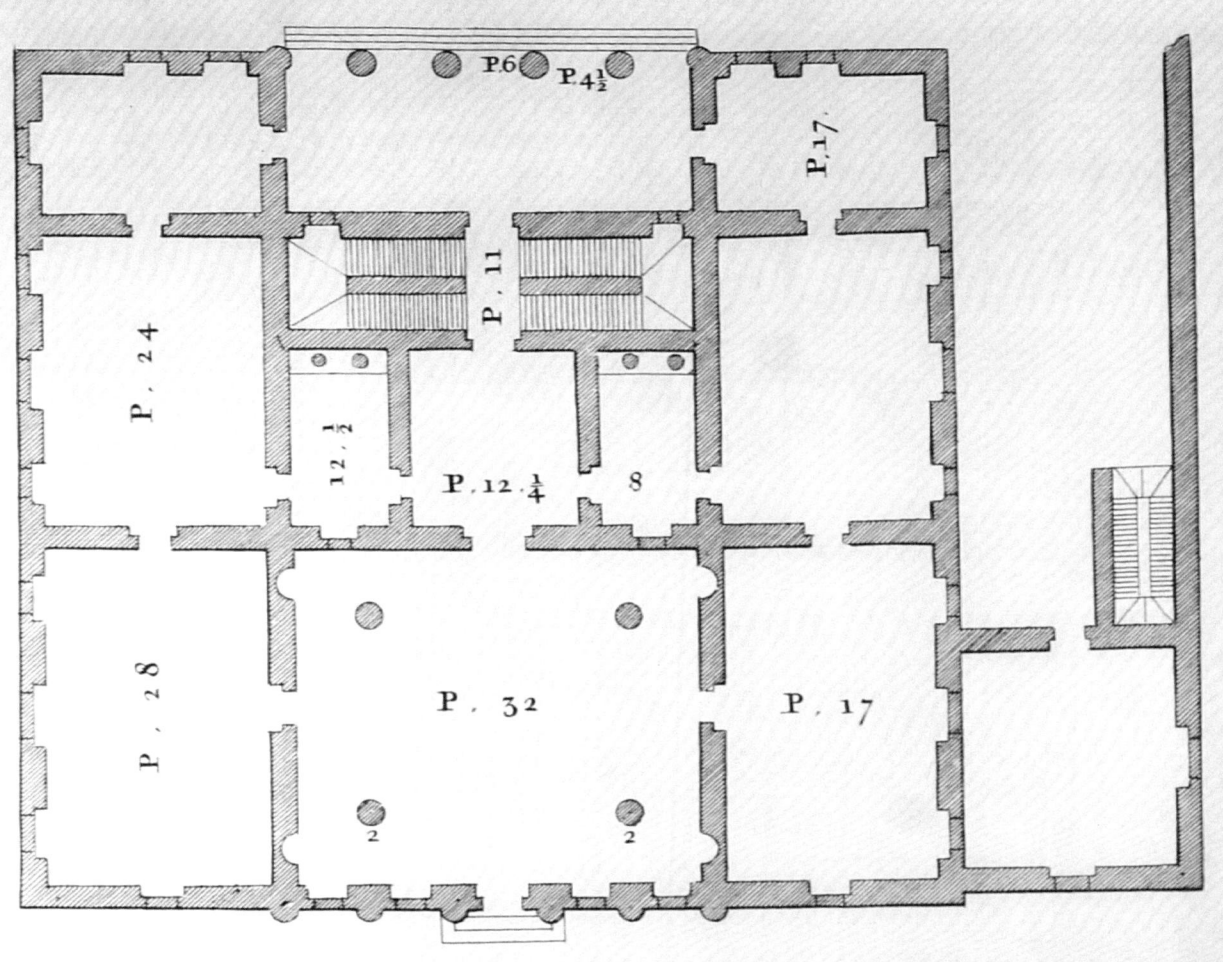

Belmont incorporated cabinet rooms similar to those developed by Andrea Palladio in the 1500s. The individual specialized rooms were becoming fashionable in America in the 1850s. (Book 2, Plate 1, from *The Four Books of Andrea Palladio's Architecture*)

spacious second story aligned with the gallery floor and then out, adding approximately six feet to the structure's width. By raising the ceiling, and increasing the width of the room, Adelicia Acklen gained abundant space to utilize the room for larger groups, making it one of the most sizable formal dining rooms in Nashville prior to the war, measuring 33'6" x 20'6."

The transition from outbuilding to dining room with kitchen below worked well from a service standpoint. A service stair, (now removed), directly outside the room on the gallery, linked the lower level with the gallery, offering easy access to both dining rooms.

Evidence located during the 1990s restoration of the "new" dining room

The popularity of billiards reached new heights in America in the mid-1800s. This rare 1850s image of the billiard room in Mentmore House, Buckinghamshire, England, provides insight into the recreational luxury such rooms provided. The house was designed by Sir Joseph Paxton for Baron Mayer de Rothschild and constructed in 1852–1854, making it contemporary to Belmont Mansion. (Roger Fenton, photographer, ca. 1858.)

confirms Acklen's kitchen building renovation occurred by the mid-1850s. Discovery of a paperhanger's signature indicates a date by which the room was in use. Paperhangers made note of their work in pencil on the east wall with the following inscription: "April 1856/by James and Benjamin Franklin/Papered this room again."[26] Depending upon how this scribbled note is interpreted it documents the Acklens' formal dining room, as it is designated today, was in service by the summer of 1856. Both existing flankers were expanded to the north with the addition of bedrooms, primarily utilized as guest rooms. With the completion of these additions the house became u-shaped, overlooking the city of Nashville below.

A second structure to the west balancing the kitchen building is of undetermined use at this point in time, though evidence suggests a billiard room was in place by the time of the Civil War at the latest. The popularity of billiards in America reached new heights during the 1840s, suggesting such a room was in use at Belmont even before the war. This space once again opened level with the gallery. Both buildings were of brick load bearing wall construction.

The broad open rear gallery abutting the north wall of the house became a connector between the house and the now incorporated outbuildings. Once adjoined to the gallery, these former outbuildings served primarily as rear wings with galleries of their own, facing each other across a u-shaped courtyard. Rooms within both wings were accessed from these side galleries. This arrangement was similar to the main house, where a majority of principle rooms opened to the rear gallery. From the newly completed u-shaped gallery Belmont appeared to be primarily one huge porch, an indulgence the Acklens and their guests would have used to their full advantage.

With phase one complete by 1853, a remarkable color change was introduced to the exterior walls. Adelicia Acklen's uncle chose to leave his natural brick walls exposed, devoid of any colored wash or paint. The mortar joints were then "penciled" drawing attention to individual bricks.[27] By the 1850s earth tones became popular, ranging in tone from deep umber to various shades of brown and a straw yellow for exterior walls. The Acklens chose a pale yellow, which survives today beneath Belmont's stucco finish. The decision to apply this color was more than a fashionable one, it became a functional necessity. By the spring of 1853, it became visually apparent exterior walls were laid of bricks from multiple years of firing. The only chance for visual continuity was the addition of a unifying color to the exterior walls.

What is most frustrating when examining Belmont's architectural history is the lack of documents to validate clues revealed by the structure. A small number of contemporary descriptions detail the impression Belmont made upon visitors. Not one bill survives from the construction period. No personal letters from Joseph or Adelicia Acklen describing the building process to family or friends have yet come to light.

By the mid-1850s Adelicia Acklen had given birth to three children with Joseph Acklen and was expecting again. Emma, the last surviving Franklin child, along with her younger Acklen twin sisters would die by the end of 1855.[28] Prior to these events, the Acklens embraced a period of peace and contentment, enhanced by a booming economy leading to sizable profits from the Louisiana plantations. Considering the building history of Belmont, dust had barely settled from one season before another project was begun. Initially intended only as a summer house, Belmont offered a lifestyle unattainable at the other Acklen homes as their entertainments continued to grow in number. The house would have begun to seem a little cramped, with an expanding family coupled with continuing rounds of guests and social obligations.

For the entire decade of the 1850s, the estate was under development in one form or another. Multiple outbuildings including an art gallery specifically designed by Joseph Acklen dotted the grounds.[29] Massive conservatories comparable to those found at either the White House or the U. S. Capitol, a bath house, a water tower, ponds and other ancillary garden structures, farm buildings, and numerous slave houses were all constructed during this period. How small could Belmont possibly have seemed in the midst of such splendor, apparently small enough to contemplate enlarging yet again.

The latest solution to perceived spatial limitations became the enlargement of existing wings with the addition of one room to the east and another to the west. Interestingly enough these new additions were stepped back from the face of the 1853 wings, just as those appendages had been stepped back from the face of the central block. This subtle but effective detail from a distance increased the width of the house visually more than it did in actuality. By increasing the horizontal footprint of the house the massive central block seemed to decrease visually in size. These additions effectively completed the five-part country house plan, so common in America for the previous 150 years.

Exact symmetry, as dictated by promoters of this classic five-part plan remained a goal of the Acklens for the final extension of Belmont. Brick was once again the primary building material and double-hung sashes were employed in the majority of window openings rather than French doors. Both new rooms were constructed with coal-burning fireplaces, identical in form to those in the central block as completed in 1853. As built the new east wing bedroom (26' x 31') could easily accommodate an entire family in one space. The west wing, as wide as the east wing, was however more shallow (26'6" x 20') than its' counterpart.

A new cast iron balcony to the rear (north) of the west wing addition overlooked the city. Access to this balcony was gained through the use of two jib doors, one located in the recently built west wing bedroom, and the other in the billiard room. This balcony, offering fine views of the city below, became an appropriate location for gentlemen to indulge in a smoke, cue stick in one hand, cigar in the other.

These last additions to the principal façade brings into discussion multiple cast iron balconies which originally encircled Belmont's wings. By the late 1850s cast iron balconies, porches, window hoods, column capitals, figural animals, statues, grave markers, and even entire fronts of buildings were manufactured in America. The Acklens likely ordered from a catalog or a retailer in New Orleans during their winter sojourn, or perhaps they ordered in Nashville. Producers of ironwork such as the J.B. Wickersham ornamental ironworks company of New York City published a catalog in 1857 for distribution.[30] As found at Belmont, iron railings and posts offer a visual lightness to the exterior, much needed to counterbalance the physical massing of the structure that is in contrast to the intended use of a light and airy summerhouse.

Belmont's painted brick walls, representing several building campaigns, no longer offered the cohesive appearance required by so large a building. The preferred material for such a substantial structure of this prominence would have been cut stone for all exposed wall surfaces. The primary hindrance to the introduction of cut stone was not the cost, but the sheer mechanics of applying a stone veneer to existing walls. Portions of Browning's original brick walls had been incorporated into the exterior of the 1853 house. The decision was made in 1850s to continue building with brick, precluding a changeover to stone without incurring even more undue expense. From addition to addition brick courses may not have been properly aligned offering a missmatched appearance.

In an effort to create a unified appearance, between 1857 and 1860 the Acklens decided to stucco Belmont's bricks walls. All exterior masonry surfaces were covered, then scored to appear as if large ashlar stone blocks composed the walls. Finally, Belmont became a cohesive whole with the application of cast iron balconies on multiple elevations, coupled with new stucco. As originally tinted, the stucco appeared to have a pinkish hue, as if the entire structure had been transplanted to the hills of Middle Tennessee from the shores of Lake Como in Italy.

The architectural history of Belmont Mansion is tied to one major American commodity produced prior to the Civil War, cotton. The rise and fall of market conditions dictated the continued development or stagnation of numerous southern farms and estates from 1820 to 1860. Joseph Acklen had a propensity for investing his wife's money well. The growth of the Acklen fortune was fostered by an expanding worldwide market desperate for bale after bale of American cotton. Few economic events adversely influenced the soundness of cotton prices worldwide. Not even the "Panic of 1857," as it swept across the United States, causing bank failures and the closure of railroads, came close to having an effect on cotton prices.

Planters in the south proceeded as if economic conditions fostering their lifestyles would continue forever. Cotton was more than king in the 1850s. As world markets expanded it appeared southern planters were not able to produce enough product to meet those demands. The Acklens were perfect examples of this phenomenon, endorsed as they were by increasing financial advantages. It must have appeared to Joseph and Adelicia as if the money would never stop in those halcyon days prior to the outbreak of war. Their lifestyle, including purchases of rosewood furniture, artworks, and numerous building projects certainly appear to have reflected this attitude.

Were the Acklens not the central characters in this history and we concentrated only upon Belmont Mansion's construction, the entire spectrum of an expansive southern economy would still be spread before us. From foundation to roof, from one wing to another, each and every architectural element is an illustration of having more money than the majority of Americans would have seen in ten lifetimes.

Surviving documents tell the story of extraordinary profits produced in Louisiana year after year, amounting to upwards of $118,000 per annum.[31] Adjusting for inflation, the same amount would be $3,551,422.52 today, all without having to pay income tax.[32] It is no wonder Belmont was continuously expanded and improved during this period. At some point the question surfaced for the Acklens of how and where to spend the money. Much of what they expended in the 1850s, short of increasing land holdings in Louisiana, led to the further development of their Belmont estate.

Americans of this era were an interesting lot, fiercely independent of foreign states, but possessing a slavish devotion to cultures left behind. Attitudes, coupled with a sense of entrepreneurship, led people to believe they too could live in palace-like surroundings. Throughout history the accumulation of wealth has continuously propelled individuals to a higher social status. Belmont became an attraction for visitors of a certain distinction for whom the doors were always open. The social ambition of one partner in the Acklen marriage was balanced by an interest in politics and business by the other.³³ Belmont became the perfect stage from which to launch these personal objectives.

However, by the late 1850s these goals were problematic, for Belmont lacked a substantial space in which to entertain. Elevated numbers of guests were not a major consideration in the fortune building years of the early 1850s. An oversized opulent space was now required, as suddenly the house became too small. Certainly, not too small in which to live, but too small for activities required in order to further their personal success. The time was right it seemed to expand once again.

Moving forward with another expansion required a perfect plan, for Belmont had already been expanded in every direction possible, or so it seemed at the beginning of 1859. To solve this quandary a fashionable local architect was consulted. Adolphus Heiman, born in Prussia, was conversant in the latest, most up to date styles of architecture. Adelicia Acklen and Heiman first crossed paths with the death of Isaac Franklin in 1849. Heiman had been involved in the construction of an Egyptian Revival style mausoleum at Fairvue, in which Franklin and his children were buried.

Since that time Heiman's career exploded, considering the lengthy roster of structures with which he is known to have been associated. Churches, hospitals, university structures, commercial buildings, a bridge crossing the Cumberland, a theater, a Masonic Hall, Nashville City Hall, the Giles County Courthouse, and numerous private homes were part of his contribution to Tennessee's antebellum architecture. By September of 1850 *The Daily Evening Reporter* said of Heiman he was "so well known that a word of praise would be superfluous."³⁴ Heiman, to the pleasure of his clients, worked in several popular styles of the day, Greek Revival, Gothic, or Italianate coupled with an ever present hint of Classicism.

The Acklens turned to Heiman in 1859 to design what was to become the final addition to Belmont. It was decided to enclose a portion of the U-shaped courtyard to the rear, thereby creating a much needed entertainment space. Complications with this plan would have been apparent from the very beginning. The life enhancing rear gallery, the heart and soul of early Belmont, would be lost by this solution, in combination with the upper gallery as well. Enclosure of these galleries would preclude the movement of cooling air to the interior. A splendid view of the city below would disappear with the construction of a new rear wall. A reworking of the gallery would also entail redesign of the 1853 stairs.

Heiman's design found solutions for all concerns in a deft and balanced manner. Primarily, there was no better place for the new entertaining space than at the base of the u-shaped house formed by the gallery and the wings. As constructed the salon answered the need to be a communication space adjacent to other formal areas of the mansion. The formal dining room, billiard room, and central parlor originally opened into this new room, allowing for large crowds to circulate from room to room.

Heiman understood architectural principles of proportion and balance, well evidenced in his 1859–1860 addition to Belmont. The salon was to be three times as deep as the now incorporated gallery. Maintaining the historic ceiling height of the gallery would have been claustrophobic to the design. Proportionally, had the accepted height been maintained, the room would appear much smaller than its actual size (58'x 28'6"). Heiman wisely arched the ceiling to a height of 22' creating a massive barrel vault, one of the architectural glories of Belmont. With the assistance of Heiman, the Acklens created one of the largest rooms of any domestic interior in the state prior to the Civil War. Only Rattle and Snap, the George Washingtom Polk home in Maury County, comes close to having a room of comparable size.

To encircle the salon at the height of the old gallery ceiling, Heiman designed a classically detailed, multi-faceted plaster cornice, featuring spread-winged eagles as the principle element. Had the ceiling not been arched in Heiman's salon, the wide multi-faceted cornice would have been ponderous and overwhelming. This is far from the fact in reality; it is now the principal element of the room. As completed in 1860 Heiman brought a more refined educated hand to Belmont than those whom had formerly been employed at the site.

A primary feature of the open Belmont gallery, now lost to the enclosure, would have been light and air coming into the house. Heiman managed to create the illusion that the new room was still open to nature by including multiple window openings to the north. Two tripartite windows, (a wide central window flanked by narrow windows) one on each side of the centrally located bay, run from floor to the cornice line on the north wall. The lower sash in these windows are each just over six feet tall. The central sash opens full height rising into a wall pocket built above the top sash. People could then pass through onto what is presumed to have been a cast iron balcony originally running the length of the room around the existing bay.[35] The three windows in the bay all operate exactly the same, again allowing access to the balcony.

This "window wall," for that is essentially how it functions, is unusual for this period in time. More typical of the 1870s and 1880s than the 1850s, this feature brought Belmont forward into another age. Heiman's tripartite windows are the most obvious Italianate feature of Belmont displaying arched sash, the tops of which contain panes of colored glass.[36] From these windows Strickland's recently completed Tennessee State Capitol could be viewed in the distance.

In 1859-1860, the Acklens completed their last addition to Belmont. The new Grand Salon measured 58' by 28'6", with a 22' ceiling. (C.C. Giers, photographer, ca. 1870, Belmont Mansion Association)

Harking back to his classicist youth in Prussia, Heiman removed a number of original square gallery posts in the center of the old gallery opposite the stair, replacing them with a column screen of four fluted Corinthian columns visually dividing the new salon from the old porch. These columns were centered on a new staircase much more fitting for the use of Adelicia Acklen's new space.

Gone was the presumably utilitarian gallery stair, now replaced with a centrally located stair within its own niche directly to the rear of the entry. Positioning of the staircase in this location increases the social and architectural significance of the new salon. The stair empties directly into the center of the old gallery, now incorporated into the salon. As it reaches the floor, the new stair bows out invitingly at the bottom, either beckoning you to rise from below or climb down as if descending from on high, depending upon your position. Flanking the stair are identical columns to those in the newly installed column screen just across the width of the enclosed gallery. Heiman's stair of mahogany, cherry, and walnut first rises in a single flight, divides at a landing into two arched flights, then curves upward to the left and right before reaching the second floor.

Adolphus Heiman's 1859–1860 Belmont additions included the now necessary cupola, a cooling device designed to pull hot air up and out of the house in lieu of an open gallery below. Acklen is known to have referred to this element as her "astronomical observatory."[37] The cupola is by far the most obvious Italianate-influenced feature of Belmont, dating it to the period of Heiman's last additions. It is octagonal in shape, ringed by pairs of French doors opening to the roof for ventilation or an evening stroll for star gazing if one so chose. A central chimney rises through the structure piercing the cupola's roof. Visually supporting the cupola's roof overhang are a series of brackets encircling the structure mounted just above the French doors.

One embellishment, likely designed by Heiman utilizing his classical background, is noteworthy as a finishing touch to the entire composition. The plain gently sloping roof supporting a wide overhang, dating from 1853, was simply too outmoded an element in combination with the now stuccoed, iron balcony encrusted façade. Heiman was known to incorporate parapet walls on other domestic projects of this period.[38] Belmont's new parapet wall was added to the existing roof structure, aligning it with the load bearing wall below. The run of the parapet wall was interrupted by a series of four plinths across the width of the central block imitating facades of ancient works. Upon the corner plinths Heiman placed classical statues. The same parapet design was also added to the wings with yet more statues reaching for the sky. This rooftop device was employed in ancient Rome, brought back into fashion by Palladio, who featured it on several designs in his *Four Books of Architecture*.

With these final additions, Belmont was complete. While one Acklen home was finished, another was being planned for which materials were then being gathered. A newspaper in Milledgeville, Georgia,—*The Federal Union*— announced on August 2, 1859, Colonel J. A. S. Acklen was anticipating the erection of a sixty-room "castellated Gothic" house on the banks of the Mississippi River in

Louisiana. This home was planned to be approximately double the size of Belmont.

Joseph and Adelicia Acklen, with the completion of Belmont in 1860, possessed a most livable house, reflecting designs of centuries past and technological advances of their own time. Hampered as they were by the remains of the Browning house, a comfortable yet impressive plan was developed. Up to the time construction began in 1850, a majority of builders nationwide was mired in an ages old central hall plan. As asymmetrical designs developed with the introduction of Romantic styles, such as Gothic and Italianate at mid-century, some found it difficult, even then, to break away from more typical arrangements. The simple addition of a bay window here or there by local builders often became their only nod to current styles, perhaps with a centrally placed tower as an add-on to a plan long viewed as correct, functional, and unchangeable.

A first look at Belmont gives an impression the Acklens fell victim to these long accepted priorities. A balanced five-part plan suggests rigid adherence to the past. It is only when stepping into the entry that differences immediately become apparent. Visitors are first confronted with a small square entry, not the expected long broad passage running from front to rear containing a stair along one wall. Directly ahead a projecting chimney breast becomes the most prominent feature of the space. This area is designed for more than funneling guests from one room to another, as is the conventional entry hall. It is a space where you are meant to linger, while admiring assembled collections of artwork and statuary placed about the room.

As built in 1853, light would have flooded the room from both north and south elevations, for in essence this space was no more than a narrow hyphen joining the exterior with larger, deeper rooms to both sides. Sunlight filtered through colored glass of red, yellow, and purple in four pairs of French doors with Venetian glass transoms above. The entry opened to the exterior on both the north and south.

Should any visitor fail to recall the Acklens built a house primarily for summer use, this space would swiftly remind them of that fact. This reality led to the completed plan of 1860, no matter how large the house grew to be. With the addition of numerous rooms, the principal of cooling air and its distribution throughout the structure became a factor in each construction phase. Hence the addition of Heiman's cupola, creating a chimney effect, pulling air into, up, and through the house, thereby crafting an equivalent of a modern day whole house fan.

As Belmont continued to grow in size throughout the 1850s, one unifying element became the first floor gallery, whether it be open ended or closed, as it became by 1859. To this gallery in time

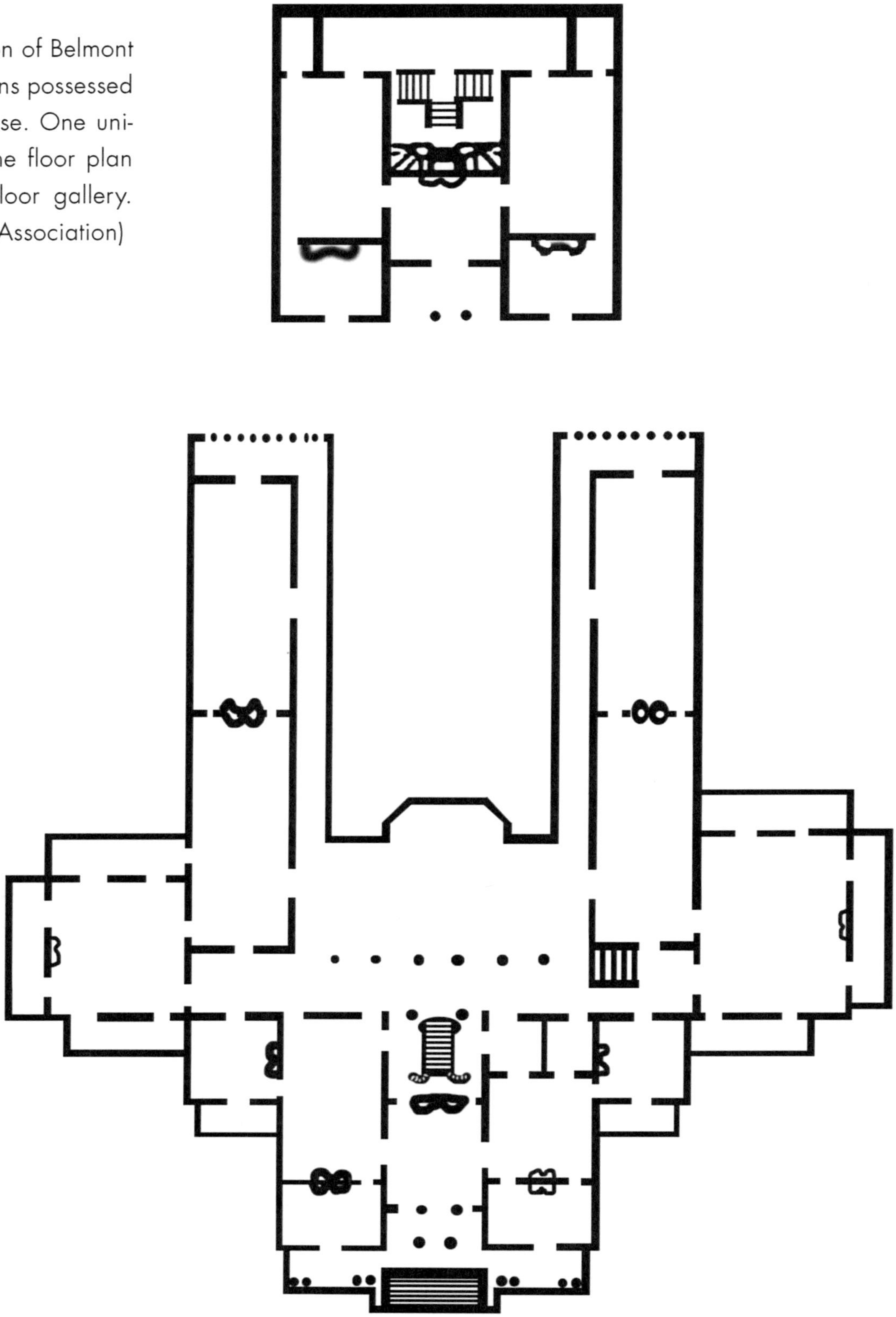

With the completion of Belmont in 1860, the Acklens possessed a most livable house. One unifying element to the floor plan became the first floor gallery. (Belmont Mansion Association)

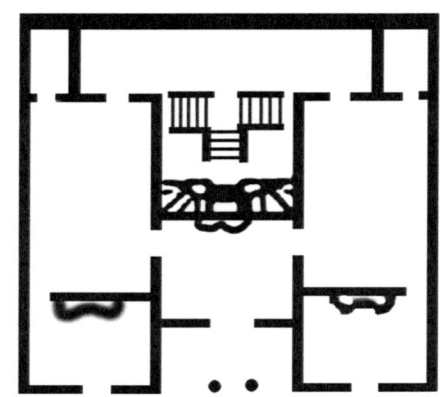

were attached a formal dining room, a billiard room, and up to four guest bedrooms, but never in such a way to limit airflow, only enhance it. Placement of these additions qualify the importance of the rear gallery for life at Belmont. From this space the majority of first floor rooms could be accessed. Serving as a passage to parlors, study, and entertaining areas, this multi-purpose space would have been one of the most heavily utilized in Belmont. Single story wings to the rear served as extensions to the principle gallery, offering cooling shade to a number of rooms within.

The French refer to rooms that are aligned in sequence with a view from one room to another as an enfilade. Belmont does not perfectly fit this description but the builder's intent was the same. All rooms on both the first and second floors connect to at least one primary space with views into others. There are no dead end spaces to be found anywhere in the house. All rooms either provide access to another room, the exterior, or access to a cast iron balcony overlooking the grounds.

With the addition of the Grand Salon in 1859–1860, the final development of Belmont's plan was in place. This concluding addition enhanced the original concept without hampering it. Heiman created a functional entertainment space reminiscent of baronial halls in Europe if only by sheer size alone. As the room with the greatest ceiling height and a wall of windows facing north, the Grand Salon served as an extension of the original rear gallery. Bedroom additions at each end of the gallery featured large French doors, allowing for cross breezes to flow through the house into the now enclosed gallery. From the first and second floor galleries, rose two stylish staircases, acting as a chimney for the transfer of hot air into and out of the new cupola.

With few exceptions, such as service and dish pantries off the library, the plan of Belmont is like an open book with one side reflecting the other. This adherence to an "old-fashioned," what some would refer to as a Georgian plan, did not in the least detract from the livability of the structure for "modern" times. Lacking a central hall, a deliberate deletion from the plan, forced the joining of all interior spaces together, opening the rooms to light and air, necessary elements for health as the nineteenth century was slowly beginning to recognize.

The comfort accorded by such a plan for a family in residence, aided by a large retinue of servants, is undeniable. With the advent of mechanical systems artificially controlling interior environments, we have lost an appreciation of homes such as Belmont, built in a time when architecture and nature could be joined in a palatable partnership. The Acklens in their time understood and made use of information we no longer choose to acknowledge.

From the beginning of construction in the spring of 1850, it was apparent to any casual observer that the house of Joseph and Adelicia Acklen, was unqualifingly unique. No other house constructed in Nashville offered such fascination, or had yet created this degree of interest among the populace. The design held nothing back, there is no reticence of detail or proportion in any aspect of Belmont Mansion. All is monumental in scope, from towering columns set within a two story recessed porch, to a multi-faceted modillioned cornice wrapping the central block, seemingly three stories high. Atop the house stands a parapet wall interspaced with plinths designed to support a series of classical statues. As if two statues on the central block were not enough, the same feature is repeated on wings to each side.

Few American homes of the era offered such visual opulence. Similar to ancient temples, Belmont could only be entered by climbing a flight of stone steps to the *piano nobile,* as the Italians referred to the principle entertaining floor. Rising before contemporary visitors, the mass of Belmont's structure would surely have been overwhelming. A two story central block projects forward from single-story symmetrical wings wrapped with cast iron balconies. Not one, but two classical porticos project from the principal façade to the right and left of the recessed entry porch. These matching elements shelter French doors topped by transoms containing etched red Venetian glass sparkling in the sun. Few homes in Nashville could boost porticos as detailed as these. Pairs of fluted columns topped with cast iron Corinthian capitals support each portico, while fluted pilasters complete the composition adjoining the front wall. Barely visible atop the house was an octagonal cupola, as fully ornamented as if it were constantly in view.

Debow's Review published a description of the estate in August of 1860:

> Mr Ackland's which we visited, is a perfect paradise, and is marked by natural beauties not to be surpassed anywhere.... Nothing is spared which one of the greatest fortunes in the country can command. The grounds are tastefully laid out, the buildings are commodious and costly.... Within the mansion are many choice and valuable paintings.[39]

The site of Belmont alone guaranteed adulation. Placed directly between two of the busiest pikes in Nashville, travelers were well aware of Belmont's existence, even if the verdant landscape allowed for only a fleeting glimpse of the mansion. Urn-topped cast iron gateposts, rising eight feet into the air, announced one would soon be crossing into another world, totally sculpted and manicured, unlike any other estate in the city. As completed in 1860 with the assistance of Adolphus Heiman we are left today with

Some have compared Belmont to the Villa Borghese in Rome, a "villa suburban" for social events. For over a hundred years, historians have attempted unsuccessfully to find a link between Belmont Mansion and the villa. (Alessio Domato, photographer, 2007, Wikimedia)

this symbol of an era representing unfettered wealth, soon to be brought to an end by war.

In 1850, few Americans could have imagined or anticipated our nation being ripped asunder in little more than a decade. What concerned most Nashvillians at the time was the increase of commerce spurred by growing trade and the national economy. Both Joseph and Adelicia Acklen were participants in these concerns. Primary evidence of this is the home they spent ten years planning and building.

Categorized in the twenty-first century as an Italian Villa, Belmont bears little resemblance to a true Renaissance villa. From the time Belmont was completed, long before the first coat of decorative finishes dried, there have been multiple attempts to describe this house, while assigning a specific structure as inspiration. Many have looked straight to Italy and the buildings of the Italian Renaissance, in particular the Villa Borghese in Rome, built by Cardinal Scipione Borghese in the early seventeenth century. Cardinal Borghese had much in common with the

Acklens. They were both rich, well educated, and collectors of artworks, but one building most assuredly did not inspire the other. Villa Borghese was in effect a "villa suburban," a building in which to primarily gather for social events, while Belmont served first as a family home and second as a showplace.

Villa Borghese was built to impress, awe, and inspire, all of which could be said for Belmont as planned by the Acklens. In essence the two structures have little in common, with the exception of the builders' intent, and the lifestyle they shared, separated by two and a half centuries. There is no common cornice line defining the mass of Villa Borghese, as can be found at Belmont. The Acklens built for light and air, while the cardinal, judging from the size of wall openings in his villa, built for privacy and the security of his collection.

The builders of Belmont were tied to antecedents of American architecture much more than they knew or would ever have admitted. The form in which they chose to build, of central block, balanced by receding wings, is strictly redolent of a classic five-part house most commonly found in eighteenth century America. Look beyond the architectural details and fenestration of Belmont to the physical massing of the structure. Do not let the abundance of blank wall space seemingly unbroken by windows and doors mislead you. What is left would have easily been recognized by Thomas Jefferson as he stood in front of Carter's Grove in 1775.

Building when they did, the Acklens expressed a desire to move toward a more popular modern style. They were handicapped however, by previous architectural experiences. In an era when classical details and symmetry were slow to give way to more romantic styles, the Acklens bowed to each era in which they lived, both the classical and the romantic. They harkened to the past, never quite being able to adopt a completely modern attitude toward the design of Belmont. Classical details abound on both the interior and exterior of the structure, in combination with a building footprint utilized multiple times by previous generations.

As they looked to the future, the Acklens continued an American tradition of requiring the latest technological advances within Belmont. America, then immersed in the Industrial Revolution, discovered it was possible to light, heat, and bring running water to the interior of a home on a more permanent basis than anyone a generation earlier would have believed possible.

The Acklens first exposure to such advancements would have come through travel. American hotels, by the third decade of the nineteenth century, offered improvements such as running water to lure people like the Acklens into their establishments. Gas lighting became available in the east as early as 1818. By 1850 Nashville was just beginning to consider forming a municipal gas company. Belmont's owners, living two miles from downtown, had no hope of being connected to a gas line for years to come. A more immediate solution exercised by the Acklens was to install a private gas plant on the property, lighting all four levels of the house, plus numerous outbuildings.

Most important was the introduction of a water tower and piping system designed by Adolphus Heiman, supplying water to the interior of the house by no later than 1859, perhaps as early as 1857. The fountain installed in the Grand Salon in 1860 is evidence of water being available within the walls of Belmont. Considering water was used for domestic as well as ornamental purposes, introduction of a recognizable bathroom within the walls of Belmont would have been paramount. Prior to that time, a well-planned system of cisterns supplied domestic water. There is no doubt the Acklens enjoyed a bathroom within the walls of Belmont by at least the end of the decade, but most likely earlier. This "convenience" would have been viewed as a "necessity" to people of the Acklens status. American homes of comparable size were rapidly transformed by the very type of advancements employed by the Acklens at Belmont.

While looking to the old world for architectural inspiration, as evidenced by the choice of the newly popular Italian Villa style, the Acklens remained firmly a part of the American school of design and innovation. Neither of the Acklens had yet crossed the Atlantic to view originals of the form they were building. Their inspiration relied primarily, as it did for others of their generation, upon published works of established eastern architects.

This not to say the Acklens made a conscious decision to build an American house, but that is precisely what they did. Utilizing a floor plan tested by the ages made for a commodious functional structure. No matter how they chose to use Belmont, as a home, a country retreat, a party palace (there is plenty of evidence to support this theory), or as a space to hold their growing collections, the Acklens' enjoyment in the process is evident by their results.

These conclusions in no way denigrate the accomplishments of the Acklens or Heiman. They built to prove it could be done. They built also, it must be said, for personal aggrandizement to a certain extent, presenting what they perceived to be a European model as the centerpiece of their country estate. They built for the ages, with much consideration given to the creation of a world different from any they had previously known. Credit must be allotted for developing an estate resembling no other in the American south in their day and time. In the twilight of an era, the Acklens produced a lasting statement of American architecture. They did what Americans have done so well since

1607 in Jamestown, Virginia, taken the best of the old world, making it function with renewed purpose for a different time and place.

1. Roberta Brandau, editor, *History of Homes and Gardens of Tennessee* (Nashville: The Parthenon Press, 1936): 130.

2. Anita Goodstein, *Nashville, 1780–1860: From Frontier to City* (Gainesville: University of Florida Press, 1989): 95.

3. Mills Lane, *Architecture of the Old South, Mississippi-Alabama* (New York: Abbeville Press, 1989): 41.

4. United States Slave Census 1850, state of Tennessee, Davidson County, 781.

5. Charles Vaughan, Jr., *George Steel: Architect and Builder of the Nineteenth Century* (Huntsville Historical Review vol. 13, January– April 1983, Huntsville-Madison County Historical Society): 5.

6. James Patrick, *Architecture in Tennessee 1768–1897* (Knoxville: The University of Tennessee Press, 1981),30.

7. Anita Goodstein, *Nashville, 1780–1860* (Gainesville: University of Florida Press, 1989), 205.

8. Mother Frances Walsh, O.P., *The Annals of St. Cecilia Convent* (Unpublished Journal of St. Cecilia Convent, 1860–1881, Nashville, Tennessee, Belmont Mansion Archives), 31.

9. John Wilson to Joseph Acklen, September 13, 1853 (Unpublished letter, Acklen Papers, Manuscript Collection 86, Louisiana Research Collection , Howard-Tilton Memorial Library, Tulane University, New Orleans, La.)

10. Photo ID 4016, (Tennessee State Library and Archives, Photo Collection, Nashville, Tennessee)

11. James Patrick, *Architecture in Tennessee*, 32.

12. Ibid., 38.

13. Thomas W. Palmer, *A Register of the Officers and Students of the University of Alabama 1831–1901* (Tuscaloosa: University of Alabama, 1901), 41.

14. Elizabeth Fries Ellet, *Queens of American Society* (Philadelphia: Charles Scribner & Co., 1867), 418.

15. Joseph A. S. Acklen, Journal of J.A.S. Acklen c. 1832–1834 (Nashville: Belmont Mansion Archives).

16. Mills Lane, *Architecture of the Old South-Georgia* (New York: Abbeville Press, 1986). 144.

17. David Morrison, the most talented of this genre, was a native of Pennsylvania. He first arrived in Nashville in 1828, worked locally until the mid-1830s, then appears to have moved west to Memphis.

18. Latrobe is known to have designed an unexecuted plan for Senator David Campbell as related in *The Domestic Architecture of Benjamin Henry Latrobe* by Michael Fazio and Patrick Snadon.

19. James Patrick, *Architecture in Tennessee 1768–1897*, 132.

20. Belmont Mansion, *Adelicia Acklen's Life in Chronological Order* (Belmont Mansion Archives).

21. Various historians and architects have examined this structure from the 1970s forward. Everyone from Henry Judd of the National Park Service to architect James Patrick (*Architecture in Tennessee 1768–1897*) has agreed Belmont was developed over a period of years involving several different building campaigns.

22. Anita Goodstein, *Nashville 1780–1860* (University of Florida Press, 1989), 205.

23. On-site architectural investigation conducted in July 2016 revealed walls and chimney breasts were dovetailed into existing walls of the original house (Browning era), suggesting many structural changes in 1850.

24. Andrea Palliadio, *The Four Books of Architecture* (New York, Dover Publications, 1965) Second Book, Plates I, XXXI, XXXVI, XL, XLV.

25. James A. Hoobler, *Cities Under the Gun* (Nashville, Rutledge Hill Press, 1986).

26. Belmont Mansion, Belmont Mansion Room Files, Room 116. [Ed.: Much of the structural history of the Browning house and its successor Belmont has been revealed by Stephen W. Brown and Paul Hoffman, Republic Building Conservators.]

27. George T. Fore, unpublished exterior finish analysis report, 1985, 3.

28. Laura and Corinne Acklen, born in 1852, succumbed to scarlet fever in the spring of 1855.

29. William Hayes Ackland, *Scion of Belmont: William Hayes Ackland Recollections, 1855–1878* (Chapel Hill, William Hayes Ackland Papers, Southern Historical Collection, University of North Carolina Library).

30. J. B. Wickersham, *Victorian Ironwork* (Philadelphia, Athenaeum Library of Nineteenth Century America, 1857 Catalog of 1857, reprinted 1977).

31. Belmont Mansion Archives, Adelicia Acklen's Life in Chronological Order, March 12, 1851.

32. Bureau of Labor Statistics Annual Consumer Price Index.

33. As listed in Belmont Mansion's archives Joseph Acklen became active once again in politics by 1856 when he served as a member of both the state and national Democratic conventions. Prior to his marriage he had served as the district attorney for Northern Alabama.

34. James Patrick, *Architecture in Tennessee 1768–1897*, 146.

35. Structural evidence still exists in the form of attachment points on the exterior suggesting the existence of a balcony in this location. The windows would not have been designed to open from the floor had they not been intended to provide access to a balcony from the salon.

36. Samuel Sloan, *Sloan's Victorian Buildings*, originally titled *The Model Architect* (New York, Dover Publications, Inc. 1980 reprint of 1852 edition) design X: pl.XLL, fig. 2

37. William Hayes Ackland, *Scion of Belmont: William Hayes Ackland's Recollections, 1855–1878* (Chapel Hill, William Hayes Ackland Papers, Southern Historical Collection, University of North Carolina Library), 3.

38. This same element is utilized on several houses attributed to Heiman, all the same period as Belmont—Fatherland, Ashwood Hall, Riverview, and Elmwood.

39. *DeBow's Review,* (New Orleans, August 1860, vol. IV), 248.

"Making a Display"
Adelicia Acklen's Tennessee Family Portraits

By Rachel Stephens

Certain expectations were placed upon antebellum women in the American South, namely modesty, and quiet strength even in the face of unspeakable loss. Adelicia Hayes Franklin Acklen Cheatham (1817–1887), known as Adelicia Acklen today, owned nineteenth-century Nashville's most impressive art collection, and she used it to communicate these characteristics. The collection included an interesting mix of white idealized marble sculptures, European masterpieces—both originals and copies, and dozens of family portraits by Tennessee artists. It was eclectic to say the least, and there was nothing else comparable in the region. In her time, family portraits were common in the homes of wealthy Tennesseans, but her residence had excessive numbers of these. In sheer volume, even with the large assemblage of European art aside, Acklen's collection was unparalleled in antebellum Tennessee, except perhaps by Andrew Jackson who had a personal artist. The presence of so many family members' portraits in her home offers a tangible example of Acklen's devotion to her family. The conservative form and style of the work also falls right in line with dominant artistic trends in nineteenth-century Tennessee. Despite the fact that Acklen collected art from around the world, her family portraits, which helped many of her children's legacies live on past their premature deaths, were perhaps the pride of her collection.

The opulence of Belmont during Acklen's years there between its construction in 1853 and the 1884 sale at the end of her life not only reveals the expansive nature of Acklen's tastes but her acute cultural awareness as well. Much meaning can also be drawn from the Tennessee family portraits in particular. While her

Adelicia Hayes Franklin Acklen Cheatham owned nineteenth-century Nashville's most impressive art collection, including a large number of family portraits. (C.C. Giers, photographer, ca. 1870, Belmont Mansion Association)

family portraits served as mementos, certainly painted primarily for personal pleasure, these works also helped Acklen proclaim and justify her rightful place among the best Tennessee and southern circles. Belmont mansion was a site of entertainment, and the portraits, painted mostly by Tennessee artists, helped remind visitors that Acklen was not only a member of an old and important Tennessee family but that she cherished her large family circle as any proper southern lady would. As art historian Lauren Lessing notes, "Through the tasteful elaboration of their domestic interiors, middle- and upper-class Americans also hoped to define themselves favorably and reinforce desired aspects of their identities."[1] Acklen's identity was something she hoped the family portraits would favorably reinforce. Her persona was called into question in some circles and throughout different points in her life, and her Tennessee portraits, proudly showcased throughout her home alongside her European collection, helped her define herself in traditional and acceptable modes. In addition to family members' portraits, multiple images of Acklen herself appeared throughout her home. In these, she chose to represent herself in modest roles and as a loving mother.

During her life, Acklen often stepped outside of limits that were typically placed on antebellum Southern women. She was fiercely independent, a characteristic at odds with proper bounds of nineteenth-century femininity. Mary Telfair, for example, an unmarried and highly educated Savannah elite once noted that, "Alexander [Telfair's brother] seems to think I will be too independent for a Lady."[2] Despite, or perhaps because of her unconventional actions, Acklen filled her home with conventional (if abundant) portraits of her family by Tennessee artists. Therefore, despite the opulence of her tastes, which revealed itself elsewhere in her art collection and throughout her estate, in the family portraits, she stuck to the local traditions and thus aligned herself with other elite Tennessee families. Hung throughout the home and considered together, these works were carefully commissioned over the years to present specific messages about Acklen and thus to place her within what was considered to be her proper place in society.

Acklen was born in 1817 and came of age alongside the city of Nashville. Steamboat travel into the city became available in 1819 and this encouraged a period of growth and development.[3] Nashville had been selected as the capital of the state in 1843, and the cornerstone for William Strickland's grand capitol building was laid July 4, 1845. By 1861 Nashville was serviced by five railroad lines. The city fell to the Union in 1862, which it fortified, and the United States Army occupied the town throughout the war. Nashville, like Acklen herself, came out of the war in a somewhat enviable position. Certainly the war had taken a toll on the city, but it was not decimated as others in the South were.

According to historian Don Doyle, "Of all major southern cities, Nashville emerged from the war with fewer physical and political scars and with advantages gained in the war that prepared it for a formidable role in the new order of things."[4] Similarly, Acklen's vast accumulated wealth, still in place at war's end, provided her advantages that she continued to enjoy throughout her life.

Like her art collection, Acklen's reputation was varied. She was a reigning Nashville socialite, and among the wealthiest people in the South, but she received her fair share of criticism as well. She was born and raised among the elite in Nashville, but some of her actions caused her to be criticized by both local residents and visitors and, at times, left her feeling like an outsider. Certainly the vast wealth she acquired as well as her lavish lifestyle at her Belmont estate set her apart. Her fierce independence also separated her from other female members of her elite class. Historian Catherine Clinton discusses the lack of control of movement and decision-making that most plantation matrons of the planter class maintained in the antebellum era. As she describes, "the planter had come to dictate her identity as well as her dependency."[5] Unlike most women of her class however, Acklen seemed to dictate her own identity and make decisions for herself. Her overt financial motivation was one source of criticism, and this idea guided many of her decisions.

It could be argued, for instance, that she married her first husband, Isaac Franklin, because of his personal fortune, despite the fact that much of it was gained through his successful slave trading business. He was also undereducated and nineteen years her senior. A couple of accounts exist as to how the pair came together, but each of them have a twenty-two year old Adelicia Hayes expressing romantic interest in the fifty year old Franklin while she was visiting his 2,000 acre plantation in Gallatin, Tennessee.[6] Franklin, who was one of the wealthiest men in the state, died only seven years into their marriage. Ultimately unsatisfied with the terms of his will, she and her daughter contested it, and eventually won the lion's share of Franklin's estate even though he had dictated it for use in the establishment of a school that was never formed. According to her youngest sister Corinne Hayes Lawrence, "She could talk a bird out of a tree."[7]

Shortly after Franklin's death, Adelicia began acquiring property of her own, including a home in downtown Nashville that she kept throughout her life, as well as the huge tract of land on which Belmont would sit. Coming into her second marriage to Joseph Acklen with a personal fortune, she stepped outside of traditional female bounds by signing a prenuptial agreement with Acklen, thus giving her and her heirs complete control of her assets. The Acklens constructed Belmont on the property that she had independently acquired. In her third marriage to Dr.

William Archer Cheatham, a similar marriage agreement was finalized. In the most notorious example of Acklen's criticized independence, after her second husband, Joseph Acklen's death during the Civil War, Adelicia, assisted by a female cousin, travelled to Louisiana from Nashville in an attempt to sell their cotton, rather than risk having it burned by the Confederates. The ultimate sale of this cotton to England (which netted her a fortune) from Louisiana during the Civil War involved negotiating with both the Confederate and Union troops, and she was rumored to have engaged in careful manipulation of each side in the process. She had taken control of this affair in the wake of her husband's death, and she realized the significance (both personal and financial) of the matter. After all, Acklen had written to her not long before his death, "I have nothing left now but my cotton and it is uncertain if I shall be permitted to dispose of it. I am in constant dread of its being burned." She had probably longed for the cotton to be sold because he also noted that, "my only chance of support is to sell my cotton and as soon as I can accomplish that I shall start for Nashville."[8] Acklen's death from sudden illness prevented him from ever making the trip home, however. Although Joseph Acklen may have never been criticized for attempting to sell his cotton out of the Confederacy, as a woman, this action drew suspicion and criticism on Adelicia Acklen. In a final independent move, in advanced age, Acklen took the bold step of separating from her third husband Dr. Cheatham, selling her beloved Belmont, and relocating to Washington, D.C.

Acklen's extravagant tastes, seen in the construction and evolution of the Belmont estate, were also a source of condemnation. A nun at the nearby St. Cecelia Convent cited a supposedly oft-repeated phrase: "If the Acklen fortune were exhaustible, it would have long since been consumed by its lavish owner."[9] Furthermore, a daughter of one man whom she was courting after the death of Joseph Acklen wrote, "She is a complete woman of the world and very fond of making a display of her wealth, which is very parvenuish I think."[10]

Belmont Mansion was initiated in 1853 as an Italianate style summer retreat for the Acklens. However, by 1860 the family had commissioned leading Nashville architect Adolphus Heiman to expand and remodel the structure, including the addition of a Grand Salon, and the home became the family's primary residence. Acklen had overseen construction of Belmont with her new husband Joseph Acklen after the two were married May 8, 1849.[11] Historian Eleanor Graham described the European influence on the estate, much of which could also be said of her art collection: "While some ideas were borrowed, the resulting layout is largely original, surprisingly comprehensive and interesting, with artistic balance."[12] Surprising features included a waterworks with moat, a bear pit, a bowling alley, a zoo, a 105-foot brick tower, an art gallery, as well as a vast series of underground pipes that provided plumbing for the entire property. In constructing a home two miles outside of downtown Nashville (the Acklens also owned a city residence), the family became some of the city's earliest suburbanites, a class that was reserved in its earliest form for only the wealthiest people because it necessitated private transport. As streetcar service expanded in Nashville closer to the end of the nineteenth-century, this move became possible for a greater number of people, but was still limited to the wealthy. At the height of its existence, a painting of the mansion and grounds was completed and an engraving of it appeared on an 1860 map of Nashville and Edgefield. As the engraving reveals, Belmont mansion became "the show-place of Nashville," as one English visitor noted saying, "wherever I went in Tennessee I was sure to hear of this beau ideal of splendour."[13] A member of the Dominican sisters who opened the St. Cecilia Academy for girls in Nashville in 1860, Mother Frances Walsh, agreed, saying "the Acklen place always offered objects of interest."[14] The home was so much more extravagant than anything else in Nashville, that it became known to some as "The Acklen Folly."[15] A Union soldier described it in the same vein as a "speciality in the way of extravagance."[16] Perhaps escaping the sorrow of losing her husband, the Civil War turmoil, and repercussions of her bold move in selling the cotton, Acklen took her children to Europe for a time at the end of the Civil War. For much of the rest of her long life, Acklen lived primarily at Belmont. After separating from her third husband, Dr. Cheatham, she sold the estate a few months before her May 1887 death.

Acklen's growing art collection only served to further the grandeur and paradox present in the estate at Belmont, a home beyond compare in the South. Acklen is unique in many ways, and her art collection is no exception. Most Tennesseans were interested exclusively in displaying family portraits in their homes rather than commissioning or collecting other genres, and Acklen's taste in art certainly included such portraits but also ranged far beyond them to include a wide range of European works including history, religious, and genre scenes. Like the house, the art collection also received criticism. According to one English visitor, "The walls were covered with pictures and family portraits, consisting of the mistress of the house, her various husbands (she was said to have had four), and their children. Some of the copies of Italian masters were nearly as bad as the family portraits… The rooms were rather small, and the pictures so large and in such tremendous gilt frames, that they had the effect of a house insecurely built of pictures."[17] Indeed, Acklen regularly ordered the most ornate frames available from the Tennessee artists she commissioned, and many of the portraits at Belmont today are still housed in their original decorative gilded frames. Another guest in 1881 described visiting the house, saying, "I was struck with the enthusiasm she evinced in pointing out the merits of

Belmont's mansion and its grounds became "the show-place of Nashville... the beau ideal of splendor." (Detail from "City of Nashville... 1860," Tennessee State Library and Archives)

some rare painting or piece of statuary. I ceased to remember that I was in a private residence, but thought myself to some grand art gallery."[18] Indeed it seems that people did not quite know what to make of Acklen and her collection.

Acklen's commissioning of dozens of family portraits by Tennessee artists was one of the ways she attempted to align herself with the Nashville elite and join the good graces of society. One's choice of portraitist in nineteenth-century Tennessee was certainly significant, and Nashville was proud and supportive of its growing art scene. Although hiring Tennessee painters was also time and cost efficient, these things did not generally concern Acklen.

Rather, supporting local artists and displaying their works in her home would have helped bolster her local reputation much more than commissioning outside professionals. Having herself and her family depicted in the same styles as other Tennessee elites would have had a similar effect. She could have easily commissioned an artist from elsewhere, and she did do this on occasion; however, she chose to primarily stick to the known and trusted local artists for the majority of her commissioned portraits.[19]

Although some itinerant artists passed through Nashville in the 1810s and 20s, the market at that time was dominated by the city's sole resident artist, Ralph E.

W. Earl. By the 1830s, however, Earl had removed to Washington to live at Andrew Jackson's White House, and the art market opened up a bit. Native Tennessean Washington Bogart Cooper was poised to fill Earl's shoes. Cooper quickly gained the lion's share of middle Tennessee's portraiture clientele. Art historian Budd Bishop describes Cooper's "influential patrons, isolated stylistic development, and a provincial flavor" as "a perfect barometer of a developing state beautifully suited to the temper of the times."[20] Cooper became Nashville's most prolific nineteenth century artist, and his modest style perfectly suited local tastes. According to his account book, he averaged thirty-five portraits a year between 1837–1848, making his moniker of the "man of a thousand portraits" seem quite fitting. He became the most popular artist in nineteenth-century Tennessee history, and he produced many portraits for the Acklens.

As a child of distinguished Nashville parents, Adelicia had the best upbringing Nashville could offer. She attended the prestigious Nashville Female Academy with the other most prominent of the city's daughters, and she was a young student during the Marquis de Lafayette's visit on May 5, 1825.[21] Acklen was intelligent and well educated, fluent in French, and she graduated at age sixteen "with highest honors."[22] She was also familiar with the Nashville art scene from a young age. Her mother Sarah C. Hightower had sat for Nashville's first resident artist Earl and according to him, "I never had a lovelier model."[23] Acklen's parents, who were first generation Tennesseans, her father having moved there as a young man from Massachusetts to initiate a legal career, actually had a long tradition of association with local artists. Oliver Bliss Hayes became very well acquainted with Earl after his arrival into Nashville in 1817.[24] The two men became founding members of the Tennessee Antiquarian Society in 1820, the precursor to the Tennessee Historical Society. Although it is likely that Hayes also sat for Earl, this is undocumented. Later the Hayeses would sit for Cooper and others. This artistic lineage was carried on and expanded upon by Acklen in the family portraits she displayed in her home.

The family portraits were a prominent feature of Belmont and were created by a virtual who's who of nineteenth-century Tennessee painters, including Cooper and others. Guests to the home regularly commented on the portraits in particular. A newspaper account of the 1867 wedding of Adelicia Acklen to Dr. Cheatham noted that "the portrait faces that looked from the walls seemed to have been suddenly instilled with life, and looked smiling upon the happy gathering."[25]

Acklen carefully cultivated her public image and portraiture was one important way she accomplished this. Like her art collection, Adelicia was multifaceted and this view continues when analyzing the ways in which she portrayed herself in her portraits. The surviving portraits of

Clockwise from top left:

Adelicia Hayes, portrait by Washington Bogart Cooper, ca. 1834. (Tennessee Historical Society Collection, Tennessee State Museum)

Adelicia Hayes Franklin, portrait on the occasion of her marriage, Washington Bogart Cooper, 1839. (Belmont Mansion Association)

Adelicia Hayes Franklin with her horse, Bucephalus, William Browning Cooper, ca. 1840 (Belmont Mansion Association)

Joseph A.S. Acklen, miniature, John Wood Dodge, 1851. (Belmont Mansion Association)

Adelicia Hayes Franklin Acklen, miniature, John Wood Dodge, 1852. (Belmont Mansion Association)

Joseph Acklen, Jr., miniature, John Wood Dodge, 1852. (Belmont Mansion Association)

Adelicia Hayes Franklin Acklen, portrait, Washington Bogart Cooper, ca. 1850-1855. (Belmont Mansion Association)

Acklen herself, commissioned throughout her life, are quite telling and depict her in various guises including as a young bride, an accomplished equestrian, a devoted mother, and a widow in mourning. Her first portrait was probably taken in 1834 by Washington Bogart Cooper upon the occasion of her engagement at age seventeen to Alphonse Gibbs, a graduate of Harvard Law School and the son of an influential Nashville family. Cooper would go on to become Acklen's preferred artist, for whom she sat multiple times throughout her life. This first striking and simple portrait depicts the beautiful dark-haired Adelicia Hayes in half length and wearing a simple off-the-shoulder black dress. Originally, Acklen appeared in the portrait in a white dress, typical of engagement portraits. However, she was devastated when Gibbs died suddenly during their engagement, and at some point the dress was painted black to reflect her sudden and deeply felt loss.[26]

Acklen waited five years before she decided to accept a marriage proposal again, and this time Cooper received another commission from her on the occasion of her marriage to Isaac Franklin. The image depicts the now twenty-two-year-old Adelicia in a three-quarter length view with a bouquet of roses on the table behind her arm. Not only did she love flowers, but they were common in portraits of young women and symbolized delicacy and fecundity. Her dress is finer than many others seen in Tennessee portraits of the period, although still not as ostentatious as something that might be seen in the less conservative cities of Charleston or New Orleans. The gauzy gown is gathered at the bust and her arms are visible through the lace on her sleeves. Her hair is parted conservatively in the center and lays flat against her head and away from the milky-white skin of her décolletage. Aside from a bracelet with garnet stones, she wears no jewelry. In her marriage to Franklin, Adelicia had come into a household of substantial wealth and this marriage portrait certainly reveals her as a woman of means. Even so, the portrait might still be considered modest and no more showy than comparable Tennessee portraits.

Acklen sat for at least one other portrait during her marriage to Franklin. *Adelicia Franklin with Horse Bucephalus* was the largest and most stunning and involved portrait yet. The work was created by William Browning Cooper, younger brother to Washington Bogart Cooper, who ultimately became a popular painter in Memphis. The portrait depicts Acklen with her beloved horse Bucephalus, whom she named after Alexander the Great's horse. She also owned a bronze statuette of the horse. Acklen was noted for her superior equestrian skills. Her great-granddaughter remembered, "Unlike some ladies, grandmother liked to take the reins and drive even the most spirited animals," and it was said that she would rather jump over a closed gate than stop to open it. This grand work reveals Adelicia in one of the roles in which she took great pride.[27] This portrait also comes closest to representing her strength. Typically, however, she chose to display images of other historically strong women in her home, rather than herself, and these included the Cumean Sibyl, Judith, Hagar, and Queen Victoria.

As Acklen's wealth grew, interestingly her portraits became more modest. The pride the Acklens placed in their family unit can be seen in a touching trio of images, perhaps the most personal of all of Acklen's portraits. In 1851 and 1852 John Wood Dodge created three miniature portraits that depict Joseph Acklen, Adelicia Acklen, and their first child at age 2, Joseph Hayes Acklen.[28] These works represent a model of domestic harmony according to nineteenth-century standards. Joseph Acklen appears upright and strong, while she seems steady and feminine.[29] Her milky white skin was a sign of refinement. Little Joseph Hayes Acklen's round miniature is typical of the period as children were often shown as if protected in their angelic innocence by a bed of clouds. Although nothing is known about the commissioning of these works, miniatures are intimate portraits, usually given as gifts in recognition of the personal bond between sitter and recipient. Perhaps the Acklen works were gifts between husband and wife. The first miniature appears in Dodge's account book on November 3, 1851, as "J. A. S. Acklen, one hand." The price was $125, paid in cash. A year later the portraits of "Mrs. J. A. S. Acklen" and Joseph appear in Dodge's account book for $125 and $75 respectively, making this trio among Dodge's priciest works.[30] Perhaps Joseph Acklen first commissioned his own miniature as a gift to his wife, especially in light of their regular periods of separation, and Adelicia returned the favor the following year.

Together these objects comprise a popular form of portraiture in mid-nineteenth century Nashville.

According to one newspaper article from 1840, "If a portrait is wanted, Mr. Cooper is the artist—but if a miniature be preferred for mother, wife or "ladye love" call upon Mr. Dodge."[31] After apprenticing to a sign painter in his native New York at age sixteen, Dodge (1807–1893) gained some training at the National Academy of Design, and by the early 1830s had established himself as a popular miniature painter. He lived in New York until the late 1830s when failing health caused his doctor to advise him to head south. After first spending time in Huntsville, Alabama, Dodge ultimately settled in the larger city of Nashville by May 1840.[32] Nashville remained his base of operations for the next twenty-one years.[33] Dodge was a successful and popular miniature painter from the start, and he found ready patrons and quick work in Nashville. Miniature painting is a tedious and unforgiving medium and Dodge excelled at it. His miniatures were generally of the larger mode, 2 ½ or 3 inches high, and were often intended to be hung around the neck. They were expensive items, usually costing between $50 and $100 each.[34] Because miniature portraits were an extravagance, Dodge painted the most prominent people (who had the most means) in Tennessee. According to collector Raymond White, he "painted the *haute monde* of Middle Tennessee."[35] He had limited competition and there were no other resident miniature painters of his abilities in Nashville.[36] A handful of miniature painters had traveled through Nashville by the 1830s and the region's first resident artist, Ralph E. W. Earl, who resided in Nashville full time between 1817 and 1830, was known to have painted more than one, but Dodge dominated the market.[37]

Another modest portrait of Adelicia Acklen, in which she wears a lacey black dress, was produced by Washington Cooper, probably in the early 1850s. The sensitive portrait bespoke the loss of loved ones that was too common in Acklen's life. By the time this work was created, Acklen had probably already buried her first husband and at least two children. The work is similar in many ways to Cooper's earlier portrait, on the occasion of her marriage to Franklin. Here she appears again, this time as a mature woman in three-quarter length view with her hands folded in her lap and swags of red drapery behind her. Unlike the mansion itself, the work is subdued. Acklen's hair is neatly parted and combed back, as usual, and she wears no jewelry.

Like Acklen, her three husbands also sat for portraitists throughout their lives, as most Tennessee men of prominence did, and Acklen displayed these in her home as well. Perhaps the continued presence of these works in Acklen's home was intended to remind viewers that she was twice widowed (in addition to losing her fiancé before they were married). Acklen had married Isaac Franklin in 1839, and by the time of their marriage, he had already sat for Earl. Later Washington Cooper produced several additional portraits of Franklin. The one owned today by Belmont Mansion was created in three versions by Cooper. The work depicts Franklin in the typical manner of a Tennessee gentleman, seated in half-length in a black jacket against a dark backdrop. Perhaps it was commissioned upon the occasion of their marriage as a pendant to the wedding portrait of young Adelicia Hayes Franklin. Seen with Franklin's portrait, Adelicia sits in a complementary pose, seeming to look lovingly across the canvas toward Franklin who stares outward with a bright expression. Her youth in comparison to Franklin is evident and her white dress denotes the occasion of their marriage.

Adelicia's second husband Joseph Acklen, who lived six to eight months a year in Louisiana managing the family plantations, was known as a man of "great energy and industry," and his portraits portray him as such. One now lost portrait of him always hung at Belmont and an 1881 visitor recalled seeing this life-sized portrait of Acklen in the front hall.[38] A surviving image by Cooper also corresponds with the standard taste of the time but

Isaac Franklin, portrait, on the occasion of his marriage, Washington Bogart Cooper, 1839. (Belmont Mansion Association)

Joseph A. S. Acklen, portrait, with family tartan. (Belmont Mansion Association)

interestingly portrays Acklen with a swag of his family tartan. Acklen was a lawyer by training from one of the oldest families in Huntsville, Alabama. Perhaps alluding to his heritage was another way to align the family with the Scotch-Irish descendants that dominated the region and for Adelicia to emphasize extended family relations.

By all accounts the Acklens had a happy marriage, and Joseph Acklen was devoted to his family. During the Civil War, he wrote home to Nashville from Louisiana to his beloved "Addie" that "to be seperated [sic] from you and the children for so long a time is a very great hardship but one I could not avoid."[39] With his business skills expanding the Acklen estate by the outbreak of the Civil War, the Acklens were among the richest southern plantation owners. The source of the Acklens' wealth, and thus the Acklens' ability to travel regularly, collect artwork, commission Tennessee portraitists, and live in complete leisure at a grand Nashville estate, must be

Belmont's front hall featured a portrait of Adelicia Franklin holding the hand of her daughter Emma, who died in 1855. The sculpture *Sleeping Children* was placed in front of the portrait, poignantly memorializing her children's deaths. (C.C. Giers, photographer, ca. 1867, Belmont Mansion Association)

acknowledged. By the outbreak of the Civil War, the Acklens owned about 691 slaves, many of them working the cotton fields in Louisiana. It was well understood in their day (as it is today) that the Acklen wealth was supplied by their Louisiana slaves. As Mother Frances Walsh wrote, "Louisiana plantations worked by numerous slaves were rich mines affording ample means to gratify fastidious tastes and princely extravagance."[40] Joseph Acklen's final letter home was written August 20, 1863. He died shortly thereafter on September 11 of an unknown illness, perhaps pneumonia or malaria.

Nineteenth-century parents regularly commissioned posthumous portraits of their children. Unfortunately, Adelicia Acklen found too many opportunities to participate in this tradition, as six of her ten children died by age eleven. From her first marriage to Isaac Franklin, she had four children, three of whom survived infancy. However, she lost her four and six-year-old daughters to illness just weeks after Franklin had died, leaving her widowed with her daughter Emma, who was just a year and a half old. In her second marriage, she had six children, four of whom survived into adulthood, although she lost her two-year-old twin girls just seventeen days apart in 1855, after which she wrote, "how lone and desolate feels the mother's heart."[41] That same year, Emma Franklin also died of diphtheria at age eleven. The images of her children thus also emphasize her role as devoted mother, especially in the wake of losing so many of them at young ages. One of the grandest portraits, created by Joseph Henry Bush, which emphasized her role as mother, depicts Adelicia Acklen holding the hand of her daughter Emma Franklin, who appears to be about two years old. This life-sized portrait hung on the west wall of the entrance hall to the home while the large companion portrait that depicted Joseph Acklen hung on the east wall. After the deaths of the twins and then Emma, Acklen poignantly placed William Rinehart's *Sleeping Children* sculpture directly before it, as is shown in C.C. Giers photograph of the room from circa 1867. The sculpture was meant to evoke her deceased twin daughters, Laura and Corinne, whose names were etched in the sculpture's base.[42] The home's frequent visitors would have been greeted immediately upon their arrival by these works, and taken together they represent both devotion to family and the unspeakable loss Acklen had endured. They thus surely helped evoke sympathy for the widowed mother.

Commissioning posthumous portraits seems to have become a regular form of grieving employed by Acklen. This is perhaps best demonstrated by an elaborate portrait of the Acklen children, commissioned to commemorate the deaths of Laura and Corinne, entitled *The Twins: Their Resurrection*. Although the work's location is unknown, knowledge of it remains. It was commissioned from Robert Gschwindt, an artist of European (possibly

Hungarian) descent who spent winters in New Orleans between 1854 and 1867, and who was known to have resided for periods in Nashville between 1855 and 1857.[43] He also worked as an art dealer during his time in the United States, often traveling between Europe and America, and he may have served in such a capacity for the Acklens. Created in the wake of the twins' deaths, the work probably became a cherished family possession, and it was still hanging in the Central Parlor of the mansion in 1881.[44] The large, 5' x 7' painting was described in the *Nashville Union and American* as an "elaborate and expensive… family tableau." As its description reveals, it was one of the most involved portraits Acklen ever commissioned and intended "as a memorial" of the twins. According to the newspaper description the work represented:

> the four [Acklen] children and nurse… preparing for the celebration of their mother's birth-day… In the foreground the nurse is seated with one of the twins in her lap twining a wreath for its head, while the other stands beside reaching a rose she has gathered for her sister's crown; an elder sister brings a basket laden with floral treasures and a brother on the opposite side is half hidden by the foliage, from which he is culling the choicest specimens… The artist was forced to exercise his imagination in conveying the fact of the children's death, and he has done it, thus poetically and delicately; they are first portrayed in life as described, then, in the clouds above we see the same images repeated but spiritualized, and accompanied by their guardian angels, who are guiding them to the upper world—higher still two cherubim await their coming with smiles of welcome."[45]

Perhaps to accompany *The Twins* painting, Gschwindt also created a romantic work entitled *Child's Dream* (also unlocated) in which Emma is now seen dreaming of her own death. According to description, the child appears in the work holding the hand of an angel whose other hand gestures toward heaven.

Although portraits of children were less common than those of their parents in the nineteenth century, Acklen commissioned many portraits of her children (both living and posthumous) over the years. Perhaps the most charming of all of the surviving Belmont portraits depicts Acklen's three Franklin children. This triple portrait of the three Franklin girls, Victoria, Adelicia, and Emma, was completed in 1845 by Washington B. Cooper only nine months before the death of the two eldest girls.[46] The portrait depicts the three dark-haired sisters posing together in white dresses. After Emma's death in 1855, this portrait surely became an especially treasured memento.

Acklen's commissions also ranged beyond her immediate family. Although

(top) Pendant portraits of Adelicia Acklen's parents, Oliver Bliss Hayes and Sarah Hightower Hayes, by Washington Bogart Cooper, ca. 1850. (Belmont Mansion Association)

(left) The Franklins' daughters, Victoria (b. 1840), Adelicia (b. 1842), and Emma (b. 1844), in a triple portrait by Washington Bogart Cooper, 1845. (Courtesy of Beverly Kaiser)

her mother (and possibly her father as well) had earlier sat for Earl, Acklen sought portraits of them for her own household. For her parents' portraits Acklen ordered a pendant pair from Washington Cooper. The fine portraits depict the distinguished couple well dressed and in the typical mode of Tennessee portraiture. Both mature individuals appear seated in three-quarter length poses. Sarah Hayes's portrait resembles Cooper's last portrait of Adelicia from the 1850s and perhaps they were commissioned together to complement one another. According to Lessing, "Southern domestic ideology placed a greater emphasis on extended family and social relations."[47] The presence of these works would have placed Acklen, in the eyes of her visitors, within her excellent family lineage. The works also bespeak her strong family connections. The Hayes portraits are still hanging in Belmont mansion in their original gilded and decorative frames. Other works present in the home functioned similarly. Joseph's mother Elizabeth Hunt Acklen appears in a portrait attributed to Huntsville artist William Fry. Adelicia's grandparents, Joel Hayes, Jr., and Mary Bliss Hayes were also featured, as well as her brother Richard Hightower Hayes, who was killed in a duel as a young man.[48]

Through a life that seemed dominated by the loss of loved ones and in which women were not encouraged to think or act independently, Adelicia Acklen maintained her strength and forged a unique path. She flourished as an independent force in a patriarchal society in which women typically held very little power, legal or otherwise, while shrewdly managing seemingly limitless assets, maintaining control over her life, and making her own decisions. In the series of portraits she commissioned of herself and her loved ones, she presented a family heritage that likened her to genteel Tennessee society. That these portraits were significant to her is underscored by the multiple insurance policies that Acklen took out to protect her personal property in 1881. She signed up for thousands of dollars of coverages from multiple agencies, some of which was specifically purchased to cover "paintings and engravings and frames thereof."[49]

Although this brief study only offers a small sampling of the portraits of Belmont, ultimately these works are significant on many levels. Primarily, they provide a tangible visual record of a remarkable woman and her much-beloved family. Placed throughout the house, they depict Acklen and her family in the modest portrait styles that were fashionable. They stand in opposition to her less than modest reputation in some circles and reveal the elements of her identity that she probably cherished most—her role as a mother, her loss of loved ones, her faith, and the significance of family in her complicated life. Acklen's strength in the face of frequent death still rings today in her collection, which is steadily making its way back to Belmont Mansion. Acklen's cherished Thomas Sully portrait of Queen Victoria is perched over the central stair, while Rhinehart's *Sleeping Children*, the memorial to her twin daughter sits in the Front Hall. The centrality of these themes of strength and loss, and indeed Acklen's significance in nineteenth-century culture, was not lost on curators at the Metropolitan Museum of Art, who today have arranged Sully's portrait in the same space as a similar sculpted memorial to children, Thomas Crawford's *The Babes in the Wood*.

1. Lauren Lessing, "Angels in the Home: Adelicia Acklen's Sculpture Collection at Belmont Mansion, Nashville, Tennessee," *Winterthur Portfolio* 45:1 (2011): 30.

2. Cited in Catherine Clinton, *The Plantation Mistress: Woman's World in the Old South* (New York: Pantheon Books, 1982), 12, from Mary Telfair to Mary Few, 1 December no date. Few Collection, Georgia State Archives, Atlanta.

3. See Anita Goodstein, *Nashville, 1780–1860: From Frontier to City* (Gainesville: University Press of Florida, 1989).

4. Don Doyle, *New Men, New Cities, New South: Atlanta, Nashville, Charleston, Mobile, 1860–1910* (Chapel Hill: University of North Carolina Press, 1990) cited in Christine Kreyling, "Nashville Past and Present," produced by Nashville Civic Design Center, 8.

5. Clinton, *The Plantation Mistress*, 15.

6. Both stories are recounted in Albert W. Wardin, Jr., *Belmont Mansion: The Home of Joseph and Adelicia Acklen* (Nashville: Belmont Mansion Association, 2005), 3–4.

7. Vited in Wardin, *Belmont Mansion*, 1.

8. Joseph Acklen to Adelicia Acklen, August 20, 1863. Acklen family papers, Manuscripts Collection 86, box 2. Louisiana Research Collection, Tulane Library, New Orleans, Louisiana.

9. Sister Aloysius Mackin, "Wartime Scenes from Convent Windows: St. Cecelia, 1860 through 1865" *Tennessee Historical Quarterly* 39:4 (Winter 1980): 413, from Mother Frances Walsh's *Annals of St. Cecelia Convent, 1860–1881*.

10. Cited in Lessing, "Angels in the Home," 39 from Wardin, *Belmont Mansion*, 27.

11. Eleanor Graham, "Belmont: Nashville Home of Adelicia Acklen," *Tennessee Historical Quarterly* 30:4 (Winter 1971): 355. *Teresina in America*

12. Ibid, 354

13. Therese Yelverton, *Teresina in America* (London: Richard Bentley and Son, 1875): 250; 252.

14. Mackin, "Wartime Scenes from Convent Windows," 413.

15. Cited in Wardin, *Belmont Mansion*, 11 from Mother Walsh's *Annals of St. Cecelia Convent*.

16. Cited in Wardin, *Belmont Mansion*, 14.

17. Yelverton, *Teresina in America*, 250–252.

18. "A Lovely Spot: A Correspondent's Visit to the most Beautiful and Delightful Home in the Sunny South," *Louisville Courier-Journal*, May 18, 1881, 6.

19. Acklen does refer to a portrait of herself in Paris in her will, for example. That work is unlocated. She did also commission artists that regularly worked in New Orleans, such as Robert Gschwindt. Mark Brown, email correspondence, July 8, 2016.

20. Budd H. Bishop, "Three Tennessee painters: Samuel M. Shaver, Washington B. Cooper, and James Cameron." *The Magazine Antiques* (September 1971), 432–434.

21. Graham, "Belmont," 347.

22. Cited in Wardin, *Belmont Mansion*, 3 from *George Hayes of Windsor and His Descendants* (Buffalo, 1884), 102–106.

23. Cited in Graham, "Belmont," 347. This work is known through a photographic reproduction at the Tennessee State Library and Archives and pictured at www.tnportraits.org.

24. As shown by letter of recommendation by Hayes for Earl, September 15, 1820 (two let-

ters), Jackson Papers, Tennessee State Library and Aarchives, 3:14.

25. Cited in Wardin, *Belmont Mansion*, 29 from 1867 newspaper clipping in scrapbook in possession of the late Dr. Mack Wayne Craig.

26. This conservation information was provided by Mark Brown in email correspondence, July 8, 2016.

27. Graham, "Belmont," 355.

28. Raymond D. White, "John Wood Dodge and Portrait Miniatures in Nineteenth-Century Middle Tennessee," *Tennessee Historical Quarterly* 59:1 (Spring 2000): 20–37.

29. These ideas are explored by Lauren Lessing in "Angels in the Home," 31–32.

30. See Dodge's account book in John Wood Dodge papers, available in reproduction at the Archives of American Art.

31. *Nashville Whig*, June 26, 1840. Clipping found in the John Wood Dodge papers at AAA.

32. The Huntsville *Southern Advocate* of February 28, 1839, noted that after a visit of a "month or two" Dodge was leaving soon. They also noted that "we have never had an artist in this place whose pictures would bear a comparison with his… we wish a speedy and perfect restoration to health and unlimited professional success to our dear friend." cited in Raymond D. White, "John Wood Dodge and the Portrait Miniature," *Antiques* (November 2003): 152–157.

33. His presence in the city was announced in the May 28, 1840, *Republican Banner* of Nashville. Cited in White, "John Wood Dodge and the Portrait Miniature," 157. White, "John Wood Dodge and Portrait Miniatures," 24, reproduces the notice, which states that he "would be happy to execute… Miniature Likenesses, which in point of correctness of resemblance and high finish, shall compare with those of any artist in America."

34. White, "John Wood Dodge and the Portrait Miniature," 155.

35. White, "John Wood Dodge and Portrait Miniatures," 26.

36. White, "John Wood Dodge and the Portrait Miniature," 156

37. For information about some of these early miniaturists see, White, "John Wood Dodge and Portrait Miniatures," 27–29, Earl painted at least one miniature of Rachel Jackson for Andrew Jackson. He also copied a portrait of Jackson by Andrew Corwine in miniature form. The work was sold at auction by Neal Auctions in 2013.

38. *Louisville Courier-Journal*, May 18, 1881, page 6. "A Lovely Spot: A Correspondent's Visit to the most Beautiful and Delightful Home in the Sunny South"

39. Joseph Acklen to Adelicia Acklen, August 20, 1863. Acklen family papers, Manuscripts Collection 86, box 2. Louisiana Research Collection, Tulane Library, New Orleans, Louisiana.

40. Mackin,, "Wartime Scenes from Convent Windows ," 413.

41. Adelicia Acklen to Mrs. John Heiss, February 1855 cited in Graham, "Belmont," 358.

42. Lessing, "Angels in the Home," 49.

43. For more on Gschwindt, see John A. Mahé, II and Roseanne McCaffrey, eds. *Encyclopedia of New Orleans Artists, 1718–1918* (New Orleans: Historic New Orleans Collection, 1987), 166–67.

44. According to descriptions in "A Lovely Spot: A Correspondent's Visit to the most Beautiful and Delightful Home in the Sunny South" *Louisville Courier-Journal* May 18, 1881, page 6.

45. Description from undated clipping from *Nashville Union and American* provided by Mark Brown, Director and Curator of Belmont Mansion.

46. Washington Bogart Cooper Account Book, 1837–1846. Mf 100. Tennessee State Library and Archives. The work was placed on permanent loan to the mansion around 1998 from Mr. And Mrs. Franck Kaiser.

47. Lessing, "Angels in the Home," 38. See Clinton, *The Plantation Mistress*, 36–39.

48. The details of these portraits are unknown.

49. Acklen family papers, Manuscripts Collection 86, box 2, Louisiana Research

Collection, Howard-Tilton Memorial Library,
Tulane University, New Orleans, Louisiana.

GROUNDS OF "IMPROVEMENT"
The Belmont Mansion Garden

BY JUDY BULLINGTON

On a warm August night in 1884, Adelicia Hayes Franklin Acklen Cheatham (known to history as Adelicia Acklen) sat down to compose a letter to her son William Acklen who was traveling to New York. She wrote, "We all took a stroll in the grounds this evening," and indicated her son was especially missed during these walks.[1] Since the fifteenth century, the term "grounds" described an enclosed, or otherwise set apart, portion of land marking it as a special place. Grounds and garden, terminology used interchangeably in nineteenth-century correspondence, denoted a literal and figurative cultivation of space within the broader landscape whether situated in a bustling urban or pastoral country setting. Artificially shaped and ornamented grounds served as a private setting for leisure activities—such as the Acklen family stroll—and instructing young people about the natural world while providing a framework of cultivated nature within which public viewers could reflect upon the refined architectural aspects of the residence itself. Gardens were also sites for experimenting with exotic plants, innovative grafting practices, and improvements associated with the horticultural arts. Therefore, gardens functioned as the collective embodiment of a scientific mind, cultural knowledge, and socio-economic status. But they were also uniquely suited to expressions of individuality and taste. Few things could speak to the virtue of one's character better than a well-appointed garden.

Landscaped estates were built on the foundations of wealth, culture, and refinement; all of which Adelicia and her second husband Colonel Joseph Alexander Smith Acklen possessed in abundance. The newlyweds attended to the design of the gardens as an integral part of the building of their Italian-style villa from the initial phase of construction between 1849–1853. Adelicia continued to manage the gardens, including post-war renovations, following Joseph's untimely death from fever in the fall of 1863 until the estate was sold in 1887. Belmont was built on a tract of land purchased by Acklen prior to her marriage to Joseph Acklen in 1849, creating a summer home with grounds that were meant to be distinctive from working plantations

The ornamented grounds of Belmont cascaded down from the mansion in three large circular designs toward a 105-foot-tall decorative water tower. (Photo from water tower, ca. 1870, Belmont Mansion Association)

like Angola, the Adelicia Acklen's cotton-producing estate in West Feliciana Parish, Louisiana. Belmont was, in many respects, a place near family and friends where the Acklens could retreat from the demands of a planter lifestyle, which provided the economic means of building a country estate while simultaneously serving as an emblematic statement of the prominent social standing of its residents. The "situation" of Belle Monte (Italian for beautiful mountain) was particularly ideal in terms of the splendid vistas it afforded from atop one of the highest hills near Nashville. The grounds in front of the mansion, facing away from the downtown view, were laid out in three large circular designs that cascaded south down the slope toward a 105-foot water tower and nearby greenhouse.

The Acklens' garden was created during a pivotal period in early American garden history. Andrew Jackson Downing's publications—notably his popular 1841 first edition of "A Treatise on the Theory and Practice of Landscape Gardening Adapted to North America"—were dispensing how-to advice to individuals who had "an attachment to a certain spot, and a desire to render that place attractive."[2] The beauty of the spot as elegantly cultivated in the taste of Adelicia and Joseph Acklen offered captivating "prospects" for family, friends, and the pleasure-seeking public given access to the grounds every day of the week with the exception of the Sabbath. Visitors could amble along pathways covered with gleaming white clam shells transported from the coast of Louisiana, meander through colorful floral beds, repose in blossom-covered gazeboes, or contemplate the classical and animal statuary that ornamented the grounds. Formal landscaping covered approximately sixty of the 177 acres of the estate, while kitchen gardens—essential for meeting the needs of family, guests, workers, and nearly three dozen enslaved people—lay outside the cultivated frame of the baronial-like garden.

Involvement in the design and development of the garden appears to have been a collaborative effort on the part of both Joseph and Adelicia Acklen. Nonetheless, both labor and expertise were required. No fewer than nine gardeners attended to the grounds of the estate over the course of two decades.[3] It was a common practice to advertise for gardeners with French, German, or Irish backgrounds since various European countries were thought to produce professionals with the skills and expertise essential for successful gardening.[4] Leon Geny, who arrived from the Alsace region of France in 1858, was perhaps the best known gardener locally since he gained American citizenship, and his descendants established themselves in the community as professional gardeners and florists. German-born Robert Kunze was listed in the 1860s census as living with Geny in the gardener's cottage on the grounds. Post-Civil War gardeners include William C. Rock (ca. 1864–1865), William Blair (ca. 1865–1867), English-born Henry Gray (ca. 1867–1869), the Scottish-trained Owen Sharkey (ca. 1869), Elias Winkler (ca. 1870), German-born Valentine [Fischer] Fisher (ca. 1880), and Mike Mullins, who transitioned from "laborer" to "gardener" around 1870.

Belmont's gardeners participated in professional organizations and sponsored exhibitions. The June 17, 1868, edition of the *Nashville Union and Dispatch* lists Belmont gardener Henry Gray as a contributor to the first floral exhibition of the Tennessee Horticultural Society held in the Masonic Hall on May 19 and 20, which featured 672 exhibited plants. Gray received a first premium for a variety of fuchsia over Owen Sharkey who, at the time, was the gardener at the Tennessee Insane Asylum. The premiums were reversed, however, in the *euphorbia splendens* category demonstrating the competitive nature of horticultural exhibitions. Gray also won first premium for twenty-one other plant varieties he submitted to the exhibition, as well as first premium for his cut flower arrangements, "a pyramidal bouquet and a Latin cross, composed of the finest and rarest of flowers..." His won numerous second premiums and certificates as well. (Owen Sharkey still did well, however, winning twenty-three first premiums. And he became Gray's successor at Belmont.)[5]

Booksellers, like Hagan and Bro. located on Market Street in Nashville, carried an extensive inventory of publications on agriculture, including fruit and floral companions, landscape gardening for dwellings, vine-dresser's manuals, and treatises directed to men and women. William N. White's *Gardening For the South* was among the noteworthy new arrivals listed in a local newspaper on April 1, 1857, illustrating the type of printed resources available to the Acklens and their gardeners.[6]

While publications and periodicals, including A. J. Downing's complete 1855 volume titled *The Horticulturist*, graced the shelves of the Belmont's library, only select aspects of the advice disseminated within their pages were put into practice. The formal terraced-style of eighteenth-century villas that inspired earlier plantation gardens along the banks of the James River in Virginia continued to hold sway throughout the antebellum South. However, the naturalistic mode favored in modern English landscape design was gradually embraced and adapted. Yet, it would be erroneous to imagine gardens were designed solely in an older formal style or newer naturalistic mode. Period gardens were combinations of both. Landscape authors Rudy and Joy Favretti point to one such example near Nashville. "Some estates had a very straight and majestic approach, such as Andrew Jackson's Hermitage. His wife's garden had many features of the ancient style. Yet other parts of the Hermitage landscape incorporated informal groupings of trees."[7] Similarly, visitors made their way to the Acklens' villa along a road lined with cedar and magnolia trees, which ran through an open deer park before reaching the arbor-studded lawn of the more formal gardens. A reporter visiting the estate in 1863 described the scene:

In the company of an officer, I rode through a beautiful country, rich in splendid groves, breezy hills and luxurious laps of valleys, until in the distance rose a stately tower—a lookout over the country round. Presently we entered the grounds and through the grandest evergreens you ever saw, magnolias, cedars and forest trees, there was a glinting of white statues. Here Hercules, there Apollo, yonder Diana.[8]

Adelicia Acklen was well acquainted with the grounds surrounding the home of President Andrew Jackson and his late wife Rachel Donelson although they predated those at Belmont by three decades. Rachel Jackson was known to have taken particular pride in the Hermitage garden which, tradition holds, was designed by the artist Ralph E. W. Earl. She exchanged seeds and plants with friends, including Sarah Dougherty Rodgers McGavock at Carnton plantation near Franklin, Tennessee. Jackson filled flower beds with new and rare plants her husband brought back from frequent trips to Philadelphia, home of the famous Bartram Gardens that, from 1810–1850, were managed by Ann Bartram Carr (1779–1858), daughter of John Bartram, Jr., who carried on the family business of international trading in seeds and plants. However, many Nashville gardeners continued receiving plant materials through foreign agents. John Thompson ordered tulip, narcissi, daffodil, and hyacinth bulbs from Holland in 1837 for his flower garden at Glen Leven, a few miles south of Nashville.[9] These were planted in a traditional formal design, with a circular bed in the center of a square infilled with smaller geometric beds. While these and many other garden models existed locally, the formal grounds surrounding Belmont were notably larger in scale and more extensively ornamented. Plant specimens were carefully chosen for the colorful enhancements and unique or exotic touches they introduced into the visual environment.

Scholarship by garden historian James R. Cothran offers an informative two-part study that identifies distinguishing features of antebellum gardens in the deep South from 1840 to 1860 and profiles the plant materials available to gardeners prior to 1861.[10] Belmont's gardens incorporated French-hedged parterres joined by sinuous tree-lined pathways for people and carriages, rare as well as familiar plants, and classical statuary into its overall design that aligned it with the same tasteful, yet conservative, aspects Cothran associated with the broader planter culture of the colonial and coastal South.

Local gardens of the antebellum period with which Adelicia Acklan was acquainted varied in size as well as design. Acklen grew up in Rokeby, the home of her father Oliver Bliss Hayes, situated amidst open fields, pastures, and forest lands. However, near the residence there were picturesque features including a vine-covered gateway and flower gardens.[11] Characteristically, there were no plantings girding the foundations of Rokeby, a trend that would not become fashionable until later in the nineteenth-century. The gardens Acklen oversaw at Belmont reflected a combination of the familiar and fashionable in terms of design, and local as well as exotic in terms of plant materials, but the grounds were exceptional; exceeding those of Rokeby in both charm and scope. Therefore, it is more enlightening to consider Acklen's gardens within a broader geographical and cultural context.

Gardens of country villas were viewed by nineteenth-century patrons as extensions of the architecture of the house, and the grounds surrounding the Belmont mansion aligned with this ideal. In a July 1853 article on "Garden Furniture" published in *The Horticulturist*, the garden was referred to as the "country parlor" and, like their indoor counterparts, outdoor parlors were well-appointed with furnishings and decorative objects.[12] Statues produced by American and European artists were available to consumers as decorative objects for gardens by the last decade of the eighteenth-century. In Philadelphia, a 1796 advertisement read: "To be sold… Six elegant carved figures, the manufacture of an artist in this country, & made from materials of clay dug near the city, they are used for ornaments for gardens… they are well burned and will stand any weather without being injured… they represent Mars, and Minerva, Paris and Helen."[13] In the mid-nineteenth century, Janes, Beebe & Co. of New York advertised villa decorations stating that "the natural beauties of a country place can be increased by hundred-fold by proper disposition of a few vases, fountains, and figurines." The growing demand for objects to create fashionable ornamented landscapes was satisfied by agents who produced, imported, and distributed a variety of objects for private and public gardens. Ornate garden benches, statuary of allegorical figures, gods and goddesses, a menagerie of dogs, deer, rabbits and other animals, either caste in metal or carved in marble, were on offer. There was also a market for Grecian urns, fountains, ornamental balustrades, hitching posts, decorative chimney tops, gazebos used as summerhouses, and even orangeries, often echoing European models but produced and consumed in the United States.

Visitors to Belmont often remarked upon the amount of outdoor art. An account, which appeared in the August 1860 volume of *Debow's Review,* described the setting as a "perfect paradise" and noted "the resources of art have, at the same time, been exhausted upon it."[14] A list of the garden statues known to have been placed in the Belmont garden shows a preponderance of iron versus marble statuary ranging across biblical, classical, allegorical, and animal subjects. Animals comprised a popular thematic category. One example is a statue, *Reclining Greyhound,* from Horatio Greenough's 1839 sculpture titled *Arno,* a marble effigy of his beloved pet that the artist created during an extended stay in Italy. Statuary and even gazeboes from Belmont can be traced to the trade catalogues of the J. L. Mott Iron Works, Janes, Beebe & Co. and its successor Janes, Kirtland & Co., J. W. Fiske Iron Works, and other manufacturers of garden furnishings of the period. A hitching post in the form of a black youth standing on a bale of cotton is the only signed example of cast iron by Wood and Perot of Philadelphia in the collection, and it is the earliest documented example of this figure in the antebellum period. A similar hitching post was illustrated as No. 547 in the 1870 Wood & Perot catalog titled *Portfolio of Original Designs of Ornamental Ironwork of Every Description.*

Casting technology involved making and assembling multiple components. In 1853, an article in *Godey's Lady's Book* offered a detailed account of the process

used by Robert Wood in the making of ornamental ironworks.[15] The author, C. T. Hinckley, described the chest of a figure on a cotton bale being broken away to reveal an iron rod running through the center of the hitching post.[16] According to Hinckley, a figure of Hebe contained fifty-four parts; a Newfoundland dog, thirty-one parts; a life-sized lion, fifty-eight parts; a crouching greyhound, sixteen parts. All of these subjects were on display at Belmont and, with the exception of a marble version of Hebe, were produced in the manufacturer's technique of casting ornamental ironwork. Curiously, Acklen's garden-gallery objects were exclusively of iron or marble although zinc castings, a more cost-effective method introduced

Visitors to Belmont often remarked on the amount of outdoor art in the gardens. Animal statuary was popular. One example, *Reclining Greyhound* (facing page), was inspired by the famous 1839 sculpture *Arno*, by Horatio Greenough (above). (Reclining Greyhound, Belmont Mansion Association, and Arno, Museum of Fine Arts, Boston)

from Prussia, were an emerging trend in 1850s America.[17] Prussian-born architect, Adolphus Heiman, who may have assumed the role of landscape designer at Belmont in addition to engineering the water tower, would have been familiar with zinc casting as a means of making garden ornaments, but this current technology was not introduced into this site.

Other garden structures and decorative statues were described by William Acklen, including a collection of vine-covered summerhouses that offered a shaded leisure space to sit while sipping drinks, reading, conversing, or taking in the view:

> In the second circle was the largest of the five octagonal summerhouses adorning the grounds. Like the other four, it was of lovely iron work so extensively used at Belmont. Roses, star jasmine, and eglantine formed coverings of color and beauty. And here too statues, copies from the Vatican, gleamed white against their background of giant box.[18]

The second circle on the grounds contained the largest of the five summerhouses, or gazebos, adorning the grounds. The central gazebo (facing page) dates to around 1853. It closely resembled a similar iron work structure (above) in an 1858 Philadelphia ironworks catalog. (1970 photo, HABS, Library of Congress and No. 703, Wood & Perot catalog, 1858)

The central gazebo, dating to around 1853, was a combination of cast and wrought iron. An 1870 catalog of the Janes, Beebe & Co. of New York indicates its style, which matched illustration No. 4; it remained popular through the Reconstruction era. The gardens were restored and improved following the Civil War and yet another pair of gazebos was installed around 1867, but they were not of local manufactory. The centers for cast iron production, particularly in the area of garden furnishings, were New York, New Orleans, and Philadelphia. Acklen had strong ties to both New York and New Orleans, but she would also have been able to mail order gazeboes such as No. 703 in the 1858 catalog of the Philadelphia Ornamental Ironworks aka Wood & Perot.[19]

The "parlorization" of the garden as a means of displaying affluence and taste was not a practice confined to the south nor the antebellum era. There were earlier precedents. General John Eager Howard, an honored Revolutionary War soldier and politician born into a family of Maryland planter elites, built Belvedere between 1786 and 1794 as a suburban home where he furnished the lavish grounds with classical statuary and garden seats for comfort and contemplation of both art and nature. By 1798, Belvedere was one of an estimated seventy plus private pleasure gardens in and around Baltimore, which established a precedent for later country seats.[20] Like Belmont, Howard's Belvedere sat on an eminence that afforded a commanding view of the surrounding landscape. A French visitor to Baltimore remarked on "a hill owned by Colonel Howard that dominates the town to the north. The mansion & its dependencies occupy the forward part while a park embellishes the rear. The elevated situation, the mass of trees, an appearance that evokes despite itself European ideas."[21] Augustus Weidenbach painted an estate portrait of Belvedere around 1858. The artist composed a view that draws our attention to the classical statuary, urns, and wrought iron garden seats, while encouraging us to associate with the ambient experiences of the man, walking stick in hand, who strolls along the curved pathway, or the little girl picking flowers, or the young boy playing in the garden.

Creating "parlors" in private pleasure gardens had precedents in the late 1700s. The Belvedere estate in Maryland is an early example. (Augustus C. Weidenbach, artist, ca. 1858, Maryland Historical Society)

This echoes in several respects the detailed account William Hayes Acklen gave of childhood memories of his mother's gardens, evoking a sense of what it must have been like to stroll through the grounds on the family's evening walks:

On either side of the front entrance of the dwelling were huge marble vases containing the slender, graceful vines of the Russelia. Passing down the stone steps, on both sides of the flagged terrace were beds of scarlet and white geraniums bordered by rows of candytuft, leading into the formal garden which lay between the mansion and the tower.[22]

Russelia, variously referred to as a firecracker, fountainbush, or coral plant, is a tropical weeping shrub with bright green foliage and colorful red blooms. Placement in planters near the house was, no doubt, intentional as russelia attracted hummingbirds. Scarlet and white geraniums and candytufts reflected the Victorian taste for a summer display of flower-filled beds with plants arranged according to height and color. William Acklen also noted exceptional features of the Belmont gardens in addition to statuary, water fountains and a famous genus of waterlily:

Beyond, in the center of the first circle, surrounded by four marble statues representing the four continents of the world, was a marble fountain. In the pool Victoria Regia bloomed, said to have been the only one ever known to have flowered, up to this time, in the northern climate.[23]

By the 1830s, water fountains had replaced sundials as the quintessential garden ornament although, as A. J. Downing wrote in 1849, due to a lack of skilled artisans, "fountains are highly elegant garden decorations, rarely seen in this country."[24] Nonetheless, tiered marble fountains, including the one in front of the mansion, were—like gazebos and statues—available through showrooms and catalogues. Fountain bowls, balusters, spouts, pans, and basins could be mixed and matched to suit a client's taste, a nod toward the Victorian penchant for the eclectic. A second fountain at Belmont, located inside the greenhouse, was topped by a menacing cobra-headed waterspout with his hood fully extended.

Groupings of statues personifying concepts such as the four seasons, four elements, four Arcadian types, and—in the case of the Belmont Garden—the four continents were common classical additions to outdoor spaces. The marble figures of Asia, America, Africa, and Europe were positioned at the corners of a square framework with a large circular fountain at the center. The continental theme was popularized through illustrations in Cesare Ripa's *Iconologia* first published in Rome in 1593. The circa 1851 Italian statues of the four continents at Belmont are identical to those in Godinton Park in Kent, England.

The earliest documented example of the four continents in America dates to the Last Will and Testament of Elias Boudinot IV who left his "four marble emblems, each being of one of the four quarters of the world," to his nephew when he died in 1821.[25] Boudinot, a Presbyterian of Huguenot descent, was twice elected to the Continental Congress. He later served in the House of Representatives, and received successive appointments as director of the United States Mint from Washington, Adams, and Jefferson. Visitors to the Boudinot mansion in Burlington, New Jersey, recount seeing marble statues representing the four continents displayed on pedestals in the grand hallway. However, as these marbles—later identified as the work of Antwerp sculptor Jan Claudius de Cock—descended through the family, they were transitioned into a garden setting.

Symbols for the four continents closely adhered to previous representations since there were no laws in place to prevent outright copying of styles and subjects. A cornucopia and other attributes denoted the primacy and prosperity of Europe while representations of Asia tended to capture more of the Near Eastern influence. Africa wore headgear comprised of an elephant head with tusks that, according to Ripa, came from a coin of Hadrian showing elephants as indigenous to Africa where they were "used in warfare to inspire wonder and terrify opponents, specifically the Romans."[26] Visual representations of America as an indigenous female emerged in 1493 alongside other illustrations in the publication of Christopher Columbus's voyages. The version in the Belmont garden corresponds with the image of America in Ripa's *Iconologia*. Similar marble figures of the four continents can be found at Rosedown Plantation in Francisville, Louisiana, where Martha Turnbull, a devoted gardener, was mistress. In 1851, she toured Europe for six months alongside her husband and daughter to visit great estates and gardens. Statuary for the Rosedown gardens, including the four continents, was selected during their stay in Italy. The placement of the statues of the four continents at Belmont is yet another indication of the global worldview of the Acklens.

William Acklen's memory of the flowering of a Victoria Regia at Belmont has not been corroborated, but photographic evidence proves this unique Amazonian plant was successfully cultivated in the gardens of the Tennessee Insane Asylum where Acklen's third husband, Dr. William Archer Cheatham, served as physician and director. Therefore, it is not beyond reason to assume the Victoria Regia was yet another trans-Atlantic element represented on Belmont's grounds as William Acklen recounts. This genus of the waterlily was brought from the Amazon to London by British plant hunters and presented to Queen Victoria. In addition to placing specimens in the Royal Botanic Gardens at Kew, the Victoria Regia was carefully cultivated at Chatsworth for the Duke of Devonshire under the watchful eye of his gardener Sir William Paxton. Chronicles of the first blooming of this genus in captivity in the duke's greenhouse captured the imagination of Victorian audiences

Prized as garden ornaments, water fountains adorned the Belmont garden. A cobra-headed waterspout guarded the interior of the greenhouse. (top) (Belmont Mansion Association)

Groupings of statues personified classical concepts such as the four continents. At Belmont, marble figures of Asia, America, Africa, and Europe marked the corners of the square around a large fountain. (bottom) (Belmont Mansion Association)

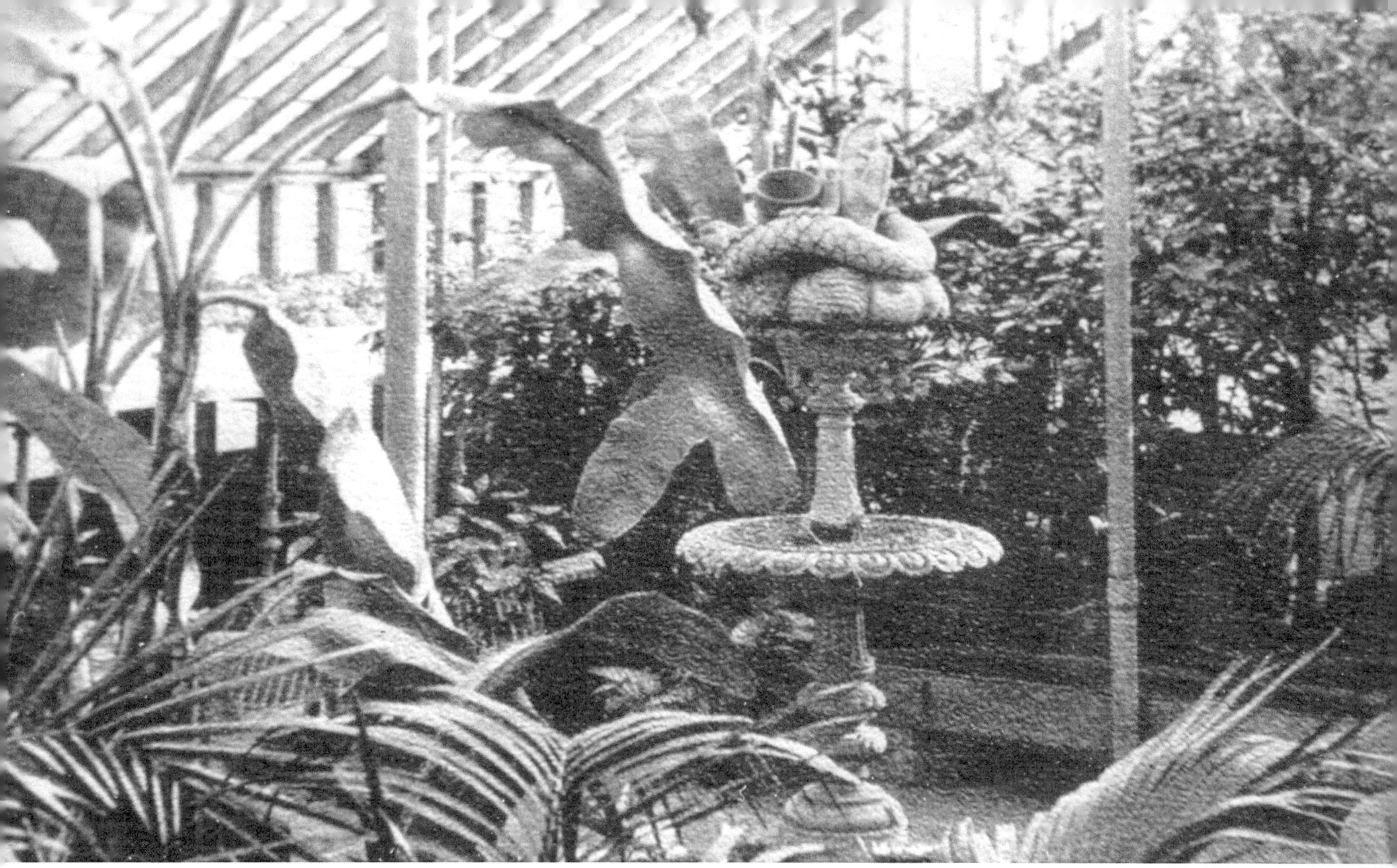

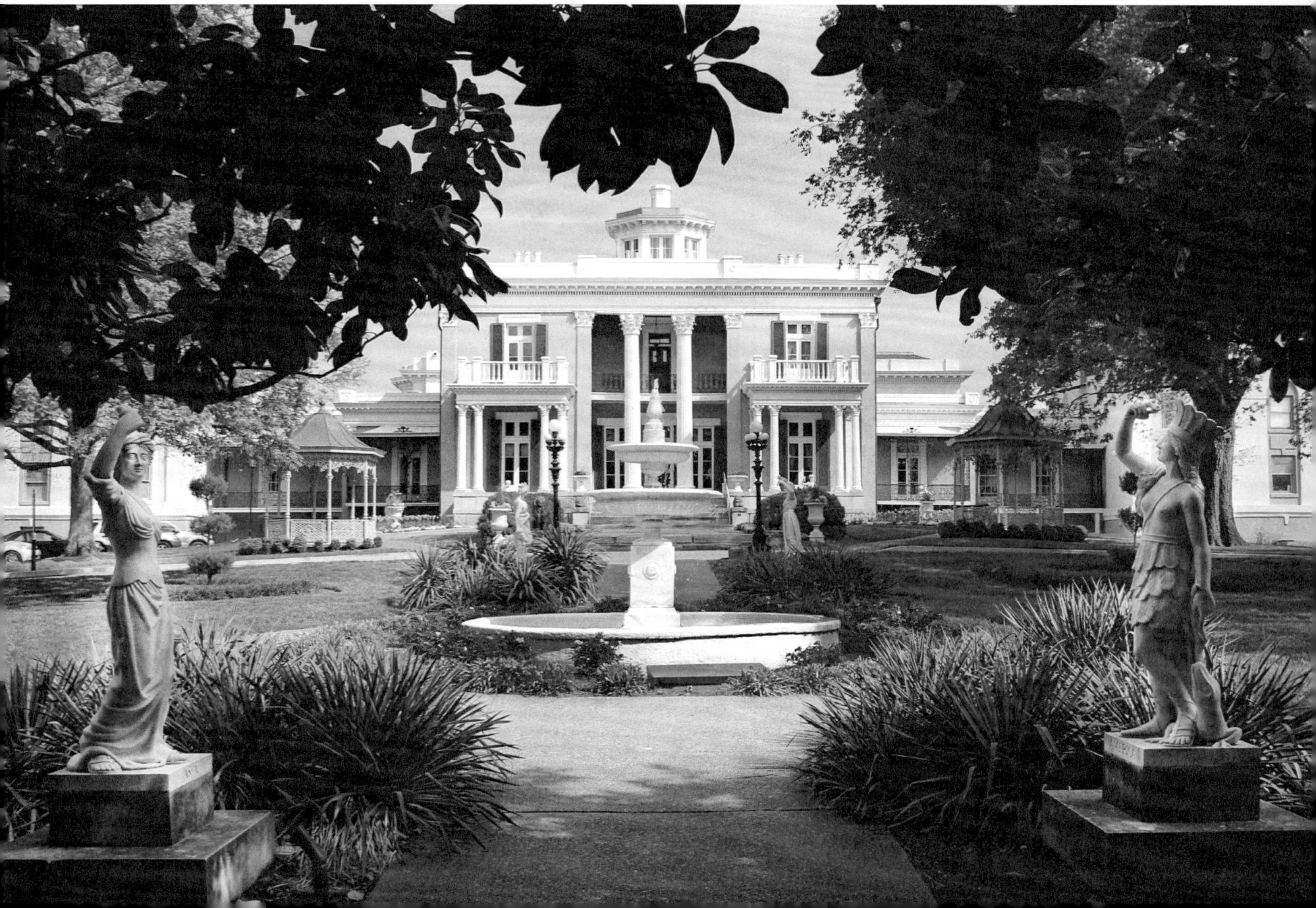

Exotic plants filled the 200-foot-long greenhouse, including banana, orange, and Indian rubber trees along with oriental palms. (Belmont Mansion Association)

internationally. The blooms measured a full foot in diameter but the leaves of the waterlily itself spanned nearly four feet; large enough for Paxton's young daughter to be photographed standing on this enormous floating pad. While the small scale of the fountain's basin referenced by William Acklen would not have allowed a Victoria Regia to reach the impressive mature scale of its English counterparts, it is possible the pool he mentions was located elsewhere on the grounds. An excerpt from the diary of John Hill Fergusson who served in the Tenth Illinois Infantry during the Civil War described "a large free stone basin about 12 feet wide and 4 or 5 feet deep" through which water was circulated by means of pipes connected to a reservoir.[27]

Fergusson remarked upon the fish in the basin, but it is feasible that the Victoria Regia was introduced into this, or a similar, stone pool at a later date.

Roses, on the other hand, were a more common feature of period gardens. We know from Sarah York Jackson's letter written in April of 1852 that the Hermitage gardens had "about fifty varieties of roses, some very fine."[28] William Acklen recalls roses at Belmont as well: "In the third circle, which was entered from the four sides through rose-covered arches, was a rose labyrinth (a miniature copy on a small scale of the one at Hampton Court), a mass of roses of all colors and varieties in an intricacy of walks.[29]

Adelicia Acklen would have been familiar with the gardens at Belair, home of the Julia Margaret Lytle Nichol, mentioned in her August 31, 1884, letter to William as having visited Belmont earlier in the day. Nichol's husband, William Nichol, mayor of Nashville 1835–1837, brought Daniel McIntyre from Scotland to take care of the garden, greenhouse, and imported plants at Belair where circular plots of lilies and triangular beds of buttercups, hyacinths, and narcissi were bordered by an assortment of annuals. Here, too, visitors could wander through the grounds on white shell-covered pathways. Exquisite rose beds were focal points of both gardens. Rose oil and rosewater had, since Roman times, been used for medicinal remedies and cooking as well as aromatic fragrances and beauty products. Julia Nichol used petals gathered from the garden to make rosewater that she bottled and gifted to guests including, one may presume, Acklen.

Greenhouse technology was essential to sustaining the estate and supporting the propagation of tropical plants. A two hundred-foot greenhouse was filled with a variety of exotics which included banana trees, Indian rubber tree, oriental palms, and orange trees. The anonymous author of the *Debow's* Review article commented that "the green-house will almost compare with that of the government at Washington."[30] William Acklen described the cluster of structures near the water tower and noted a few of the species they housed:

> The conservatory marking the lower end of the garden comprised three huge glass houses with the propagating house in the rear. In the central glass house were tropical flowers and fruits. Winter grapes supplied the family table. The west hothouse was given over to a rare collection of Camelia Japonica, some of the plants being of great age. The conservatory contained jasmines of many varieties and lilies and a fine collection of cacti.[31]

In *The Gardener's Monthly* article of January 1868 on "Horticulture in Tennessee," Fred J. French wrote, "The conservatory, built of iron, is truly a Crystal Palace, with its high dome and spacious wings. Each department is filled with costly exotics, rare and beautiful."[32] French describes the camellias fixed in William's memory as "very fine" with many being large, covered with flowers, and more than fifteen years old.

Belmont's gardens weathered the disruptions in horticultural activity brought on by the Civil War as cultivators were "called to the battleground from the garden and the spade [was] changed for the sword" while the Acklens' adjacent garden-farm Montvale did not.[33] Today only a portion of the original footprint of the formal garden and evidence of its stylish ornamentation remain within the boundaries of Belmont University's campus in the form of aforementioned cast iron gazebos, water fountains, an aviary, and numerous iron and marble statues of animal, biblical, and classical motifs acquired by the Acklens. Gardens are an ephemeral art form susceptible to seasonal changes and the winds of modernization. Unfortunately, much of what captivated nineteenth-century visitors, including a substantial greenhouse large enough to accommodate a thirty-foot Norfolk Island pine tree, must be reconstructed through other means.

In 1961, a Washington, D.C., lawyer and art collector, Max Tendler, discovered a grime-encrusted and damaged oil portrait of an unknown estate in the attic of the home Adelicia Acklen was building at the time of her death. Charmed by the painting and intrigued by the challenge of identifying the subject. Tendler had the canvas restored and then sent out inquiries to museum curators across the country. Among them was Harry Lowe, then curator of the Cheekwood Botanical Gardens and Museum of Art in Nashville, who recognized the image as a portrait of the local antebellum estate of Belmont. Today the painting, which measures 39½" x 53 ½" in its original frame, is part of the collection at Belmont Mansion. This estate portrait by an anonymous artist painted around 1860 offers a singular and detailed period portrayal in color of Belmont amidst a well-groomed landscape garden.[34] The mansion is shown perched on a hill surrounded by formal gardens complete with gazebos, statuary, and a greenhouse. Additional structures in the estate complex include an art gallery, billiards salon, and bowling alley with rooms for guests and servants' quarters, and an ice-house. The octagonal structure on the right side of the composition, originally thought to be a bear house that was part of the estate's zoo of wild animals modeled after the menagerie at Versailles, is now considered to be a bath house. Brick slave quarters and stables are barely visible through the trees in the upper right. The cupola, added to the top of the mansion in 1860, was used as an observation deck for taking in the surrounding vistas. A water tower, which appears in the lower left portion of the composition surrounded by a moat and classical statues, was under construction in the fall of 1859.[35] This is verified in a letter written by Joseph Acklen in which he states he was giving the workers a day off in celebration of the birth of the

An unknown artist captured the Belmont estate about 1860. It offers a singular and detailed portrayal of the famed house and landscape on the eve of the Civil War. (Belmont Mansion Association)

Acklens' daughter Pauline. The greenhouse and art gallery, mentioned previously, also date to circa 1860, prior to the Federal occupation of Nashville in February of 1862, and the subsequent use of Belmont as one of the Union armies' general headquarters. It is reasonable to assume this large portrait of the mansion and its grounds was painted by an anonymous artist about 1860 or 1861 after the additions to the original estate and prior to the onset of the Civil War.

What we see in the portrait is consistent with what we know about the appearance of Belmont and its grounds from this time period. Other early images of Belmont were published in contemporary illustrated magazines, newspapers, and even map legends as engravings, alongside numerous interior and exterior photographic views that can be used for comparison. An engraving of the Belmont mansion appeared on an 1860 map of Nashville. This legend image provides the clearest contemporary

The earliest known photographic image of Belmont captured a view of the villa and its garden, shot from the top of the water tower—the highest possible vantage point—by a Union soldier during the Civil War. (Belmont Mansion Association)

attribution of Adolphus Heiman as the designer of Belmont. The earliest known photographic image of Belmont captured a view of the villa shot from the top of the water tower—the highest possible vantage point—by a Union soldier during the Civil War, which enables us to see details including a horse and carriage, a child sitting on a white horse, and several people posed in the landscape. The painting from the Cheekwood collection, however, is the only known oil-on-canvas representation of Belmont. It prompts us to ask, what can an image with a partial provenance, by an (as yet) unknown artist, depicting a subject that typically resides in the margins of scholarly study, disclose to a discerning eye? Arguably, quite an abundance when it is viewed as the visual embodiment of ideals that defined the social elite of planter culture on the eve of the Civil War.

Villa and plantation portraits are related forms of "estate" portraiture. They share certain modes of representation, specifically in regards to conventions used to depict the viewer's position and direct their gaze—as characterized by John Michael Vlach in *Planter's Prospects*. The anonymous painter of Belmont used the standard portrait format identified by Vlach, which is to paint the planter's mansion from the front but slightly to one side demonstrating a familiarity with the conventions of estate portraiture. The scene is depicted from a low vantage point looking up toward the planter's home; a reversal of the magisterial gaze found in Hudson River School landscape paintings.

This shift in position directs the viewer's gaze upward, a pictorial strategy that acknowledges the deference and respect the planter class assumed as its due.[36] The foreground becomes a stage for an unanticipated encounter between two men on horseback and a figure who emerges from the grape arbor holding a cluster of fruit. The rather dramatically oversized "catbird" grapes (*Vitis palmata*) he extends to the horsemen as well as the nearby pumpkins and blueberries denote the lushness of the vegetation and the bounty of nature, functioning as outward signs of productivity and prosperity. This portion of the image coincides with the known location of a hothouse for forcing grapes which produced a bountiful supply of the fruit for the family table. But what can be inferred about the figure? The 1860 census lists the Acklens as living in the country with thirty-two enslaved individuals, (eleven females, thirteen males, and eight children), so the black man is likely an enslaved laborer and the horsemen overseers. Historian John Michael Vlach notes that enslaved individuals were rarely represented in plantation paintings made before the Civil War, although it was their labor that powered the plantation system. This was "a powerful tactic that artists used to suggest a planter's undisputed command over his estate."[37] The same tactic, it would appear, was used to depict country seats as well as working plantations. Instead of breaking with established conventions, the artist visually articulates the operative social hierarchy that existed within planter culture and establishes ownership of property.

Although Joseph Acklen signed a prenuptial agreement, he industriously set about managing and increasing Adelicia Acklen's vast holdings and became a recognized authority on effective plantation management. The decade prior to the Civil War was a very prosperous one for the Acklens, and the value of their estate increased to three million dollars. This portrait of the estate grounds not only signified their prosperity, it was an emblematic construction of Acklen's perceived skills in plantation management. A correspondent for the magazine *Southern Cultivator* wrote in 1852:

> Col. Acklen is one of the largest planters on the Mississippi River and has the finest and best managed one in the South… He employs six overseers, a general agent and bookkeeper, two physicians, a head carpenter, a tinner, ditcher, and a preacher for his negroes. The houses on each plantation are neat frame houses, on brick pillars, and are furnished with good bedding, mosquito bars, and all that is essential to health and comfort. The Negroes are well fed and clothed, and seem to be the happiest population I have ever seen. Everything moves on systematically, and with the discipline of a regular trained army. Each plantation has a hospital for the sick, well furnished; a nurse house and a general cook house…. Col. Acklen takes great interest in planting; has a fine agricultural library, and regardless of expense, keeps up with all the modern improvements in farming.[38]

The Belmont estate portrait presents gardening as a form of the overall landscape improvements the Acklens pursued through agrarian practices. The villa sits upon the crown of a hill surrounded by manicured gardens, an accouterment of ornamental objects, and an assortment of outside structures that extend and support the functionality of the 19,000 square foot main house. Although considered to be in the country at the time of its construction, Belmont afforded an excellent view of the city and river from one of the seven highest elevations in Nashville. It also had the distinct advantage of being a good distance from the swampy bottomlands that harbored mosquitoes and the threat of yellow fever.[39] The layout of the grounds, as noted previously, loosely adhered to some principles espoused by Andrew Jackson Downing, the father of American landscape architecture, who recommended clustering the more formal elements closer to the house and gradually transitioning toward a more natural arrangement. The formal garden elements are visible in the painting as a circular area rendered in a lighter color palette, which seems to pivot around an invisible axis represented by the villa. Elm trees, identified as *ulmus Americana*, bracket and control the view in a manner consistent with the picturesque landscape traditions popularized in England by Reverend William Gilpin during the eighteenth century before being adapted to American landscape design by Downing, among others.[40] Two figures, perhaps children at play, and a horse-drawn buggy provide additional picturesque motifs. The overall effect is that of pastoral serenity, drawing attention to how people who lived on, and visited this estate, were meant to experience its tranquility. Visitors who meandered along garden paths encountered edifying experiences that ultimately shaped and refined aesthetic tastes modeled on those of the privileged class who were the patrons of these constructed spaces. The fact that the Acklens were somewhat intentional about these aims is supported by their practice of opening the grounds to the public every day of the week except Sunday because Nashville lacked any public gardens at that time. This offers a tantalizing clue about how gardens, in Theresa O'Malley's view, "operated as a social stage upon which differences in class, status, and race—landowner, educated servant, and slave—were enacted and reinforced."[41]

In conclusion, gardens like those adjacent to the Belmont Mansion were artificially shaped and ornamented as a leisure space for private experience, emerging as a physiological field where bodies, material things, and well-ordered nature intersected.[42] Although paintings and other primary source images are meager documents of the actual experience of a garden environment, they function as a kind of glyphic guide to the idea of engaging nature in an "improved" form, a notion underscored by the written accounts of those who had access to the authentic grounds. Gardens, whether painted or planted, were uniquely suited to expressions of individuality and taste as well as embodying broader ideals of the time. In 1789, a noted clergyman and geographer, Jedidiah Morse, wrote of one country seat, "Its fine situation… the arrangement and variety of forest-trees—the gardens—the artificial fish-ponds… discover a refined and judicious taste. Ornament and utility are happily united."[43] The same could be said of Adelicia Acklen's gardens, which were created more than half a century later in antebellum America. The grounds of Belmont were indeed "a fine situation," where observers discovered a refined and tasteful display of cultivated nature that united ornament and utility.

1. Letter dated 10:00 PM, August 31, 1884. Ackland Papers. University of North Carolina, Chapel Hill.

2. Andrew Jackson Downing, *A Treatise on the Theory and Practice of Landscape Gardening Adapted to North America; with a View to the Improvement of Country Residences*, New York and London: Wiley and Putnam, Boston: C. C. Little & Co., 1841), 19.

3. See http://www.belmontmansion.com/estate-employees for more details. Accessed March 1, 2017.

4. See http://americangardenhistory.blogspot.com/search/label/Gardeners for background on enslaved gardeners. Accessed March 1, 2017.

5. *Nashville Union and Dispatch*, June 17, 1868. *Chronicling America: Historic American Newspapers*. Lib. of Congress. http://chroniclingamerica.loc.gov/lccn/sn85038521/1868-06-17/ed-1/seq-3/, accessed March 1, 2017.

6. *Nashville Union and American*, April 1, 1857. *Chronicling America: Historic American Newspapers*. Lib. of Congress. http://chroniclingamerica.loc.gov/lccn/sn85038518/1857-04-01/ed-1/seq-3/ accessed March 1, 2017.

7. Rudy and Joy Favretti, *For Every House a Garden: A Guide for Reproducing Period Gardens*. (University Press of New England: Hanover and London, 1990), 56.

8. "A Deer that Landseer Would Have Admired," *The Boston Daily Advertiser*. 1863. The *Boston Daily Advertiser* publishes an article apparently reprinted from the *Cincinnati Commercial* describing a Chattanooga correspondent visit to Belmont. Belmont Mansion Archive 1863/10/27.

9. Mary Daniel Brown Moore, *History of Homes and Gardens of Tennessee*, (Garden Study Club of Nashville: Parthenon Press, 1936), 165.

10. James R. Cothran, *Gardens and Historic Plants of the Antebellum South*, Charleston: University Press of South Carolina, 2004.

11. Roberta Seawell Brandau, ed., *History of Homes and Gardens of Tennessee*, (The Parthenon Press: Garden Study Club of Nashville, 1936; 2nd edition reprinted by Friends of Cheekwood, 1964), 130.

12. Peter Barry, ed., "Garden Furniture," *The Horticulturist*. 3 (8): 355–359.

13. Barbara Sarudy, "Early American Gardens: Public Gardens—July 4th Celebrations," *Early American Gardens*, July 2, 2011. http://americangardenhistory.blogspot.com/2009/07/celebrating-4th-of-july-in-public.html. (Web page no longer accessible, March 1, 2017.)

14. 1860/08, Review 1—No Title, *DeBow's Review and Industrial Resources, Statistics, etc. Devoted to Commerce*. Aug 1860; Vol IV, No. 2 APSO, 248.

15. C. T. Hinckley, "A Day in the Ornamental Ironworks of Robert Wood," *Godey's Lady's Book*, XLVII (July, 1853), 5–12.

16. For a more details see Julia Nash, "'Lacy Iron': Nineteenth Century American Ornamental Castings and Robert Wood of Philadelphia," *Pennsylvania History: A Journal of Mid-Atlantic Studies* Vol. 34, No. 3 (July, 1967), 229–23.

17. For an overview of American zinc sculptures see Carol A. Grissom, *Zinc Sculpture in America, 1850–1950*. (Newark: University of Delaware Press, 2009).

18. Quoted in Roberta Seawell Brandau, *History of Homes and Gardens of Tennessee*, (Friends of Cheekwood and the Garden Study Club: Nashville. 1964), 133.

19. An identical gazebo was sold in 1870 to the Convent of Visitation in Mobile, Alabama, by Daniel Geary, a salesman for R. D. Wood and Company of Philadelphia. Wood was in partnership with Perot from 1857–1865.

20. James D. Kornwolf and Georgiana Wallis Kornwolf, *Architecture and Town Planning in Colonial North America* (Johns Hopkins University Press, 2002), 752.

21. Barbara Sarudy, "Early American Gardens: The Practical Republican Garden in the Chesapeake," *Early American Gardens*, May 31, 2011, http://americangardenhistory.blogspot.com/2010/01/mid-atlantic-gardens-after-revolution.html. (Web page no longer accessible, March 1, 2017.)

22. Brandau, *History of Homes and Gardens of Tennessee*, 133.

23. Ibid.

24. Quoted in Grissom, *Zinc Sculpture in America*, 279.

25. Betsy Rosasco, Anne Gossen, and Elizabeth Allan, "'My Four Marble Emblems': Elias Boudinot's 'Four Continents' in Eighteenth Century America." Record of the Art Museum, Princeton University 70 (2011): 30–45.

26 Ibid., 36.

27. Unpublished excerpt copied from the diary of John Hill Ferguson, Thursday 16th. Belmont Mansion Archives.

28. Quoted. in Therese O'Malley with contributors Elizabeth Kryder-Reid and Anne L. Helmreich, *Keywords in American Landscape Design*. (Center for Advanced Study in the Visual Arts, National Gallery of Art and Yale University Press: New Haven and London, 2010), 128.

29. Brandau, *History of Homes and Gardens of Tennessee*, 133.

30. See endnote 14.

31. Brandau, *History of Homes and Gardens of Tennessee*, 133.

32. Fred French, "The Conservatory, Built of Iron, Is Truly a Crystal Palace," *The Gardener's Monthly*. May 1868 Vol. X, 137–138. Belmont Mansion Archive 1868/03/03.

33. "The Magazine of Horticulture, Botany, and All Useful Discoveries and Improvements in Rural Affairs," Vol. 29. (Boston: Hovey and Company, 1863).

34. The canvas is not signed or dated. Speculation about the identity of the artist has pointed to local Nashville painters, itinerate artisans, and even acclaimed regional painters. One possible attribution is James E. Wagner, an artist who worked in Nashville from 1840 to 1860. Wagner produced lithographs of Nashville in the years leading up to the Civil War and exhibited work at the capitol in 1858 with what the Tennessee Historical Society called "some of our very best artists." There are some similarities between Wagner's painting *Tennessee State Capitol from Morgan Park*, ca. 1857–60, and the oil-on-canvas portrait of *Belmont Mansion*. The dimensions of the canvases are comparable as are the styles of trees used to frame the focal point of the compositions. Both images emphasize figures in a landscape in a detailed foreground stage that contrasts with the architectural subjects on the hill.

35. This is verified in a letter written by Joseph Acklen in which he states he was giving the workers a day off in celebration of the birth of the Acklens' daughter Pauline.

36. Vlach provides numerous examples of this convention in paintings of plantations, including a scene from a collection of watercolor sketches made by Benjamin Latrobe as he traveled through Virginia in 1796. Latrobe's sketch depicts four viewers looking up toward a planter's home at Airy Plain in New Kent Co., Virginia, where the artist stayed for a month while recovering from an illness. John Michael Vlach. *The Planter's Prospect: Privilege and Slavery in Plantation Paintings*. (University of North Carolina Press, 2002.)

37. Vlach, *The Planter's Prospect*, 2. After the war and the abolition of slavery, Michael Vlach argues a wistful revisionism seems to have restored these people—still toiling in the service of the masters—to the landscapes they had created and on which they were so cruelly mistreated.

38. Albert Wardin, Jr., *Belmont Mansion : The Home of Joseph and Adelicia Acklen* (Nashville: Historic Belmont Association, 1981), 7.

39. Albert Bates, "A Permaculture Interpretation of Belle Monte," March 10, 2007, Global Village Institute for Appropriate Technology. http://www.thegreatchange.com/belmontwalk.htm, accessed March 1, 2017.

40. I am grateful to my colleague, Dr. Darlene Panvini, Professor of Biology at Belmont University, for her assistance in identifying some of the plant species in the Belmont Mansion painting.

41. O'Malley, *Keywords in American Landscape Design*, 26.

42. Wendy Bellion posits a similar idea for urban spaces relative to Birch's views of Philadelphia in *Citizen Spectator: Art, Illusion, and Visual Perception in Early National America* (Chapel Hill: University of North Carolina Press; Published for the Omohundro Institute of Early American History and Culture, 2011), 142.

43. Barbara Sarudy, "Early American Gardens."

Contributors

Judy Bullington, Professor of Art History and Chair of the Department of Art at Belmont University, earned a PhD in American Art History from Indiana University at Bloomington. Her research interests currently focus on an interdisciplinary study of the history of the visual arts and gardens. She is working a book-length project *Ordering Nature—Early American Artists & Their Gardening Patrons, 1760–1830*. Her awards include a Fulbright-Terra Foundation Grant (2017) at St. Andrews University in Scotland, where she is now on sabbatical.

Brenda Jackson-Abernathy is Professor of History and Department Chair at Belmont University in Nashville, Tennessee. The author of *Domesticating the West. The Re-creation of the Nineteenth-Century American Middle Class* (Nebraska, 2005), and more recently "The Civil War Diaries of William Lawrence and Kate Carney: A Research Note on Under-Utilized Sources," *Tennessee Historical Quarterly* (Spring 2014), her research focuses on nineteenth-century American women, particularly in the eras of the U.S. Civil War and expansion into the American West.

Rachel Stephens is Assistant Professor of Art History at the University of Alabama. She received her MA in art history from Vanderbilt University and a PhD from the University of Iowa. Her book, *Selling Andrew Jackson: Ralph E. W. Earl and the Politics of Portraiture* is forthcoming from the University of South Carolina Press in 2018. She is currently developing a manuscript that traces abolitionist depictions of violence in slavery and the pro-slavery response.

Jerry Trescott is the Curator of Collections at Belmont Mansion. After graduate studies at Middle Tennessee State University, Trescott began a consultancy working with historic structures, historic interiors, and decorative arts. Since joining the Belmont Mansion staff, he has contributed to the continuing restoration of that American landmark. Trescott has contributed to magazines and newspapers regarding restoration projects and he is co-author of *Carroll County: Then and Now* (2011), an architectural history of his home county in Maryland.

Guidelines
for Contributions to the *Tennessee Historical Quarterly*

1. Authors are encouraged first to submit abstracts or to discuss their article with the editor. Please send all correspondence, manuscripts, and/or aspects by email, if possible, although paper copies are acceptable if computer access is limited.

2. Once accepted for publication, final manuscripts must be submitted as Microsoft Word file via email to the editor. Keep formatting to a minimum (acceptable special codes include double-spacing, paragraph indentations, and flush left). Preferred article length is approximately twenty-five pages excluding endnotes. Text and endnotes are to be double-spaced with wide margins to facilitate copy editing.

3. For consistency, the *THQ* generally follows the style set forth in the *Chicago Manual of Style*, current edition. For matters of spelling, refer to *Webster's New International Dictionary*. Rely frequently on these reference aids. We will carefully and thoroughly edit your article, and prefer clear and accurate prose suitable for a broad audience.

4. Endnotes should be as concise as possible and conform to *Chicago Manual* style. Notes should be double-spaced.

5. All citations, quotations, proper names, figures, dates, and statements of fact should be rechecked for accuracy by the author(s) before the copy editing process begins. Wherever possible, include the full names of women, including maiden names if married. For example, do not use "Mrs. Ulysses S. Grant" but do use "Julia Dent Grant."

6. In a separate computer file, the author should submit a brief career biography (about fifty words) that includes present position, educational background, principal interests and/or current research projects, and recent or forthcoming publications. (If the article is under consideration by other journals, please do not submit it to the *THQ* at this time.) Following this, please identify the postal address, telephone/fax number, and e-mail address you prefer the THQ staff use to communicate with you.

7. Once the manuscript is accepted, the author is strongly encouraged to include illustrations (including written permission to publish from the owner) with their work. Photographs, maps, handbills, headlines, cartoons, and works of art are effective illustrative materials. These will be returned upon request.

8. If you are interested in becoming a book reviewer for the *THQ*, please contact Editor Kristofer Ray.

Correspondence regarding manuscript submissions should be addressed to:

Kristofer Ray, Editor
Tennessee Historical Quarterly
P.O. Box 89
Post Mills VT 05058
Kristofer.Ray@dartmouth.edu

The Tennessee Historical Society

Established in 1849, the oldest continuous cultural organization in Tennessee offers you the following membership benefits:

- The *Tennessee Historical Quarterly*, entering its 75th year
- Invitations to the Tennessee Historical Society fall and spring lecture series and to special events and workshops
- Special discounts on Tennessee Historical Society publications
- Free website for the Tennessee Encyclopedia of History and Culture at http://tennesseeencyclopedia.net.

------------ FOLD ALONG THIS LINE ------------

MEMBERSHIP ENROLLMENT FORM

Yes, I want to become a member of the Tennessee Historical Society.
Please [ ] enter or [ ] extend my membership in the following category:

_____ $250 John Haywood Society   _____ $45 Family or Institution
_____ $100 Bicentennial Club   _____ $35 Individual
_____ $ 75 Sustaining Member   _____ $25 Student or Teacher
(With copy of valid student ID or teacher certification number)

☐ Check enclosed   ☐ MasterCard   ☐ VISA

Name _____ Phone ( ) _____

Address _____ City _____

State _____ Zip _____ E-mail Address: _____

Card# _____ Exp date: _____

Signature: _____

------------ FOLD ALONG THIS LINE ------------

GIFT SUBSCRIPTION

I'd like to give a gift membership in the Tennessee Historical Society. My gift is for an:

_____ Individual   _____ Institution*
_____ Family   _____ Sustaining Membership

Name _____ Phone ( ) _____

Address _____ City _____

State _____ Zip _____

_____ Please notify the recipient of my gift.   _____ I prefer to remain anonymous.

* Please consider a gift membership to your local historical society or to your school or public library.

www.ingramcontent.com/pod-product-compliance
Lightning Source LLC
Chambersburg PA
CBRC092338290426
44108CB00008B/142